The Everyday Change Playbook

Because change doesn't need to be shit.

Susie Palmer-Trew

Everyday Change

Contents

Copyright	IV
1. Welcome	1
2. Problem 1) Is It the Right Change?	30
3. Problem 2) You Don't Actually Know What You're Doing	51
4. Problem 3) There's too Much Stuff Moving and Changing (Everything is Urgent and Things Are on Fire)	80
5. Things You Need to Know About That Nobody Talks About	98
6. Everyone Else's Answers to Your Change Questions	120
7. The End	127
8. What Do You Now Know and When to Use it	129
Writing is Never a Solo Affair.	140
About Us	141

Copyright © 2022 by Susie Palmer-Trew

All rights reserved.

No portion of this book may be reproduced in any form without written permission from the author, but I'll probably say yes, so do ask.

We have done our best to accurateley reference sources and contributors. If you think we have fallen short on this, we can update it really quickly, so please do just get in touch.

This publication is designed to provide accurate and authoritative information in regard to the subject matter covered. It is sold with the understanding that neither the author nor the publisher is engaged in rendering legal, investment, accounting or other professional services. While the publisher and author have used their best efforts in preparing this book, they make no representations or warranties with respect to the accuracy or completeness of the contents of this book and specifically disclaim any implied warranties of merchantability or fitness for a particular purpose. No warranty may be created or extended by sales representatives or written sales materials. The advice and strategies contained herein may not be suitable for your situation. You should consult with a professional when appropriate. Neither the publisher nor the author shall be liable for any loss of profit or any other commercial damages, including but not limited to special, incidental, consequential, personal, or other damages.

Book Cover and illustrations by Liam Willams and LeoDo

Welcome

This is technically the foreword but I'm not really into that. So, this is my welcome. It's a 'su casa mi casa' moment. This book is written for you from a commitment to write down everything we know about change and to hand it on.

> I decided to make it my thing.
>
> I am going to change how organisations change and I will do it in a way that is respectful of the people, context and capability within them.
>
> And here we are.

This book is written for the same reason Everyday Change was created, it's here to enable a better way to change. A way that you and your people can get on board with as actual real-life humans.

Openly optimistic that our experiences of change should be positive, I've made a career out of understanding change, asking people about their experiences and outcomes to then passing that learning on to those next in line. This book is one of those ways to pass it on.

It is written for a very specific audience.

- Are you trying to create change in teams and organisations?
- Are you feeling a bit lost as to where to get started?
- Are you struggling to find the real problems and priorities?
- Do you want to create something brilliant but worried it's not going to be brilliant when you get there?

IS THIS FOR ME?

So, if you nodded along to some or all of those questions then yes, it's for you.

This book is all about people (read all about you) navigating some level of organisational change. When we talk about change we mean the journey from where you are now to where you need to be. That journey can be pretty massive or it can just be you popping to the organisational corner shop because you're out of milk. It doesn't have to be dramatic, perfect or pretty. It just needs to be theirs or, in this case, yours. Best case, ours.

More importantly this book is written for those of you who have to work with what you have. Where the chance to 'bring in' the expertise is unlikely but your commitment to do the right thing by your people is on the top of your personal sticky note. It is built on practical, scalable and sustainable ideas and theory. It's been created to help you get the job done, in the best possible way for your people, your organisation and you.

Nothing in this book is unachievable. You can do everything you read with a structure that will support your planning, exploration and recovery during your change. It's all in your gift. You might need to hold your nerve but it's all yours for the taking.

> **AND HERE IS YOUR FIRST LESSON. IT'S NOT AS BAD AS YOU THINK IT IS.**

Despite what you may have read or been told changes don't just implode or cause lasting damage, haemorrhage cash and cause organisation-wide chaos. It just doesn't happen so, breathe. Let's start with some basics:

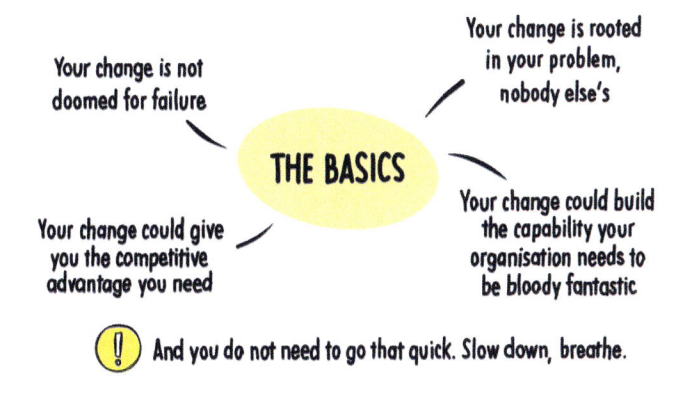

THE BASICS
- Your change is not doomed for failure
- Your change is rooted in your problem, nobody else's
- Your change could give you the competitive advantage you need
- Your change could build the capability your organisation needs to be bloody fantastic

> And you do not need to go that quick. Slow down, breathe.

- **Your change is not doomed for failure.** If you can, set some clear tolerances about what good looks like and the minimum impact you're looking for. You can set yourself up in a way that is designed to succeed. *This book will help you do that.*

- **Your change is rooted in your problem, nobody else's.** So be the expert in your needs and wants and the context that wraps around them. *This book can help guide this.*

- **Your change could build the capability your organisation needs to be bloody fantastic.** Identify what you need to win (and be open if you don't know yet) and set about lining it up, before you set off out of the starting blocks. *Reading this book is your first step.*

- **Your change could give you the competitive advantage you need.** Set the targets and create the evidence that will help you make hard decisions on the days you have to. *This book will share some ways to get you started without needing a degree in Complex Statistical Analysis.*

- **And you do not need to go that quick.** Slow down, breathe. Now start at a pace you can sustain. We *start that now with you reading this book rather than sending emails.*

A quick side note: I or we? I've not lost the plot when I switch between using I and we. When the book refers to *we* it is because I am referring to our collective Everyday Change brain made up of who we have worked with, our consultants, cheerleaders and challengers. I will use we when it's not just my opinion, or when it might feel helpful for you to know there is a gang of us rooting for you, willing you to succeed and sharing what we know to make your change better. We want to help you change your world.

How Does it Work?

This book is part 'how to' and part 'over to you'. It's designed and curated to travel with you along your change journey whether it starts next week, next year or (slightly awkwardly but highly likely) last year.

It's grounded in some great theory, theory that I actively use, teach and deliver with organisations. This is all signposted and available for you to dig deeper into. It's lifted up by practical experience and supported by the experiences of organisations and individuals who have been where you are. Because you are not the first person to be here, and you won't be the last. By building better change capability and experiences, we make it better for those affected, those who are yet to stand in your shoes and especially those who aspire to lead like you.

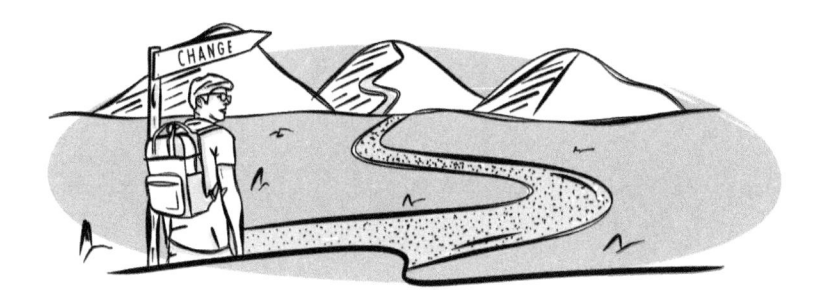

It is designed to get you to where you are heading, in a way that is right for you, your people and your organisation. We will follow a bit of a squiggly path because change isn't a perfect sequence. We'll build your change adventure together.

And it will help you solve the 3 biggest problems of change, which you may be feeling now and if not, you'll be feeling them soon:

Problem 1) Is it the right change? In this section we'll give you practical ways to identify and pressure test your change to make sure your change is right, with a clear line of sight to the outcomes you want.

Problem 2) You don't actually know what you're doing. Sorry, you weren't expecting me to get quite so brutal so quickly? Ah don't worry about it, this is all about delivering the right change, in the right way. We've all been there, whether its reality or a dose of imposter syndrome, we've got some great mechanisms, tools, stories and ideas to support you by building the best fit capability and approach that works for you, your people and your change.

Problem 3) There's too much stuff moving and changing (and everything is urgent, and things are on fire). Our organisations and people are asked to change things all the time and its tough. Combine significant change on a backdrop of day-to-day activity you're likely to make things more complicated and competitive as you tussle for shared resources and headspace. This section is focussing on simplicity, clarity and action.

Each section will give you a bit of the how and the why, with a chance to capture some of your own thoughts, have a go or come back to it later.

What's Your Problem?

Nah, we aren't starting a fight with you outside the chippy. But we want to get to the root cause of why you are here and what you need. We talk in problems.

To us problems aren't bad things to have. We use the work of Jon Hall and Lucia Rapanotti to explore problems in their purest form. A problem is a combination of a need you have and the context you are in. There is no drama and we do not need to inform Houston that we have one. But how you explore and engage in problem solving is central to what you need, how you think and where you are likely to get tripped up. And it's really important to know where you stand.

Let us start with what a problem actually is. It is a specific context with a specific need; for example if our need is accurate reporting bound by a context of regulatory requirements this is our problem. *Yeah?* Now we have a problem, we probably need a solution, or at least be on the lookout for one. **But what is a solution?** Probably more obvious, but it is 'the thing' that addresses your problem (needs+ context) that is accepted, or approved by your stakeholders. So, if we are able to find an accurate reporting widget, we have solution for our problem and if our stakeholders agree on the solution then we have a solved problem. *Still with me? Read on.*

PROBLEM
CONTEXT + NEED
SOLVED PROBLEM
CONTEXT + NEED + SOLUTION
+ APPROVING STAKEHOLDERS

How we approach change is grounded in who you are as a person and what you look for. Do you enjoy getting to grips with data and evidence, *'getting under the hood'* to prove there is a problem? Or do you quite fancy yourself as a bit of a superhero, whipping in with your cape and sorting out the solution in a flash, because *'can we just do something already?!'* ?

Because in a change situation you are likely to be one of these 'types', or at least have these preferences, where you are the same but different to you counter-part, a ying to your yang, or a 6 to a 9. Hall and Rappanotti use 6 and 9 to demonstrate the similarity and differences with a problem mindset. For those of us who are sixes we are often quick to get on, centre of the change, naturally choosing delivery focussed roles and activities, because we love a tangible outcome and progress. Our counter parts, the nine are usally adept at analysis, hypothesis and creating understanding of where you are. To make sure we are focussing on the right things, options and approaches.

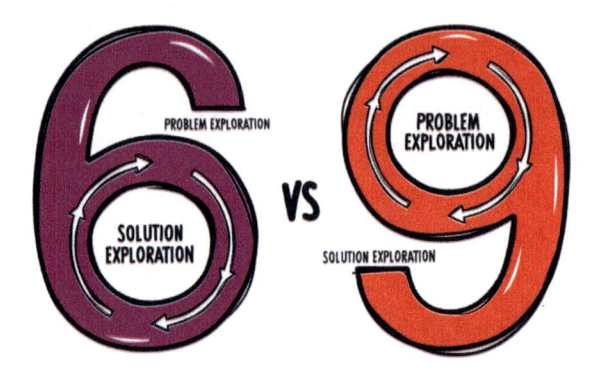

The challenge with these characteristics is that too much of one and not enough of the other won't result in progress.

If you have a room of problem people trying to progress a change I expect that you'll end up with a really well defined problem, but no solution. Counter that with too many solution people, I expect you'll end up with lots of solutions, but none will actually meet the needs of your problem, because the time wasn't taken to really understand what we are trying to do.

The answer, as with life is balance. Know who you are and then seek council from those that think differently. If you're talking to your board and you can't get them to move onto the decision on the solution, I expect you have a room of problem people (no pun intended), so ask for what evidence they need, time box discussions and move them to solution decisions. Counter that with your team, who are already off down to the shop to buy the must have solution, challenge them to provide the evidence you need before you put your hand in your pocket.

Knowing your dominant trait is as important as knowing how you feel about change, as this will influence what you do, how you work and who you need alongside you. Because whilst knowing the problem and finding the solution are both commendable we need to make sure it's the right answer, found in a timely way. And I say this knowing I am a solution person who delivers far better outcomes when the problem is clear, articulated and understood.

What is Change Anyway?

We'll keep this brief. And we aren't telling you this because we don't think you know, we are sharing so we are all on the same page.

Change is your journey from where you are now, to where you need to be. It's nothing more complicated or convoluted than that.

- You may choose to create a temporary project or team to manage that journey. That's cool and pretty standard.
- You could enable it through your day to day business. This can also work, but you'll need to be clear on what you need and what you expect so the tail doesn't start wagging the dog.
- It may need a board, or a formal reporting channel if your organisation needs assurance that it's working well (or not). If needed, try and do it within existing structures to avoid an overhead that nobody wants.

The only thing we want you to take away is that change is your unique journey. Nobody will have walked the same path, and nobody will have done it in your shoes. So be open to advice and opinions, let it all wash over you and then make decisions that are the best for you and your people.

Oh, and the most important thing about change? It's personal.

The Everyday Change Way

The basis for what you are about to read is focussed on solving or at least improving the 3 problems we see the most and how we tackle it. How we tackle it is a simple behavioural change lifecycle, built upon years (and years) of research into change and our responses to it.

It's here to help give you some guiding principles for the emotional and psychological transition from your current world to your destination. It's not perfect but it reflects our mindset, ethos and ambitions for better change. And we know from experience having something to follow is both useful and comforting, so we share this as a flow to create movement, not as a methodology to tie you up in knots.

It's not sequential or linear, depending on where you are in your change you might need to hop about a bit. We encourage revisiting areas of your change that need more care or courage. And doing so grounded in these moments gives you a clearer intent and outcomes. This is the Everyday Way.

This book is grounded in those 5 steps, or 'moments' as we like to call them, because moments aren't always sequential and they often need seizing otherwise they may feel short lived. This flow runs through everything we do, how we think, act and teach. It is not a methodology, we are creating *movement* through your change, now and how you change in the future. This book will ebb and flow through this pattern.

And these moments have expectations of you, as a change leader:

- **Resistance**: It belongs in your change and if handled with care will improve your outcomes. Don't be scared of it or get angry or disheartened when you come across it. Welcome it.
- **Intrigue**: Create it, in the adventure or the outcomes. Be openly creative and ambitious.
- **Open**: Be open to change, to feedback, to conversations, to getting it wrong, to saying well done, thank you and sorry.
- **Participation**: It's where the money is. You want this to work, create the time and space to participate.
- **Opportunity**: It won't always knock, so use your change journey to find the opportunities in the smallest of places and share them freely.

Change and the Brain

OK, quick science lesson (it's the only one). When we change, or ask others to change, we are taking on 'the brain' which is known for its tenacity and somewhat confusing messages. And whilst we all have one, its actually made of three dominant components (there's loads of other stuff, but for the sake of moving on I am sticking with 3):

- Social (Limbic) brain: helps us navigate the social world and form relationships. It is pretty opinionated and can understand what is fair (or not), can be quite judgy.

- Reptilian (primitive) brain: in charge of your vital functions; with one eye looking out for threats and danger.

- Human (Neocortex) brain: learns all the things, understands and navigates time, a calming influence on its reptilian and asocial counter parts (I can imagine this part of my brain being the voice that whispers 'calm down love')

Why a quick intro to neuroscience? When you're dealing in change, you're not talking to one person. You are actually talking to three brains that need different things.

We're talking to a brain that has learnt behaviours, expectations and plans. This brain will not spin on a pin for you, it expects you to work with what you are given, and it very much wants you to be consistent in everything you do. Because brains are brilliant, behaviours and ways of thinking are hardwired.

Contradictions are the enemy, and can be a major effort to understand, so your brain might choose to ignore it or validate what it knows to be right. You know the really annoying push back 'it's the way we've always done it' or 'it's not what we do around here'? That's your brain, protecting what it knows to be right. And when we get our way and the change goes away, or our ideas are validated. We flood ourselves with glasses of brain chemicals and we feel smashing.

For every change you ask your people to take on, you're actually asking three brains to get onboard, and they all have different needs, wants and desires and, unless what you need is in line with what they believe, you've got your work cut out.

You and Change

Easing you in slowly, we are starting with your experiences, the challenge of being a change leader and the emotional load this can create.

It's not as heavy as it sounds, we'll dispel a few myths around failure and fear and get you grounded in a change you're thinking about.

Ready? Smashing.

Why are you here?

No, not an existential question.

A big part of what comes next will be linked to your experiences of change. What you think it is, what you expect it to be and what you need it be. How you enter into this change will be based on the stories you tell yourself and the stories that reside in your organisation and the experiences of each other.

Change is often over complicated. It's never intentional, but the complexity exists in your four walls already. It's left behind by the people that went before you, the stories that are told and the consultants that seduce you with their power point slides. And it's really important that you know where you stand when it comes to your own lived experiences of change, so we know what we have to work with.

We'll start easy. Take a minute to reflect on a recent change, or a change where you know you might carry a bit of baggage. It doesn't matter what you pick, only you will know.

Let's start by focussing on the good stuff (which is often the easiest to forget).

WHEN DID IT FEEL GOOD?

And now the opportunity to have a cathartic five minutes to get down the times when it wasn't great. This is a healthy task to undertake, but it will also be your accountability partner, calling you out when any of these things, moments or instances creep into your change.

WHEN DID IT FEEL BAD?

The answers to these questions will give you the foundations for how you will create, curate and lead change. I want you to create space for them and let them take root in your consciousness. We do this to bring you some self-awareness, to keep you alert to when what you are doing starts to feel bad, so you can course correct or have a chat with a pal. I will always encourage you *to feel the feelings* not so they can hold you down, but to put them to good use, because you are about to do great things.

You can (and should!) revisit if you aren't ready to take pen to paper and don't worry (or try not to worry) if it feels hard and heavy. If you have had a bad change experience you will need time to explore and recover and if what you are going through feels rough right now then all I ask is you get some support, or at least share it with someone else, because a problem shared is often a problem halved (you can thank my Auntie Flo for that wisdom).

Are You Ready to Lead?

We've all done it, sat around waiting listlessly for a leader to turn up, to be the solution. The same often happens within change leadership. But with change, it's different; you don't need to be 'at the top', a boss, accountable for a business area. Anyone can lead change, but not everyone should.

Change leadership isn't about your day-to-day role; it's your ability to bring authority, direction and clarity to curate the momentum needed to enable your change to shine through. If you can't lead on behalf of the change, if you're protective of something beyond the change, then change leadership probably isn't for you (not right now anyway).

As a leader there is a need for you to be open to what lies ahead and that requires perseverance and patience. When I talk about being open to the change, it's about being open:

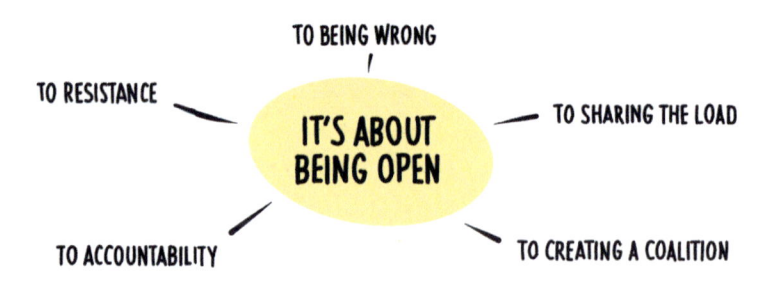

IT'S ABOUT BEING OPEN
- TO BEING WRONG
- TO RESISTANCE
- TO SHARING THE LOAD
- TO ACCOUNTABILITY
- TO CREATING A COALITION

- **to resistance**: Change resistance isn't the bad guy. Change resistance will keep you honest, adapting and on the right side of the people. So don't block it; make it safe to resist, question, and challenge.

- **to being wrong:** Our brains can be lazy, actively disrupting our thoughts is pretty hard work. We naturally look for data to reinforce our beliefs, because that feels better (and we're probably right, right?) and this stops us from seeing the world we are in and we doggedly make decisions to deliver on our individual ambitions.

- **to sharing the load by seeking expertise from the world around you:** You literally do not have all the answers and nobody actually expects you to, use the people that no better and different to improve your understanding.

- **to creating a coalition (team, gaggle, or flock):** These are the people that can deliver the change for you; advocates, experts, informal networks will set a drumbeat for your change that you could never conjure up on your own.

- **to accountability:** Do what you say, in the way you said it and be clear when you can't, won't or didn't. How you turn up for colleagues when they need you, how your meetings feel, how you communicate and take people with you will be the things those around you remember and respond to.

One of my favourite 'leadership' sentiments comes from Brene Brown who talks about needing a strong back, soft front and a wild heart. This for me is change leadership: a strong back to your change gives you clarity and stability, a soft front keeps you human, open and accessible wrapped in a wild heart keeps you courageous, curious and creative.

But if you take one thing away, change leadership isn't for everyone (and that is fine). Knowing when it's not for you could be one of the best decisions you make for yourself and for those around you.

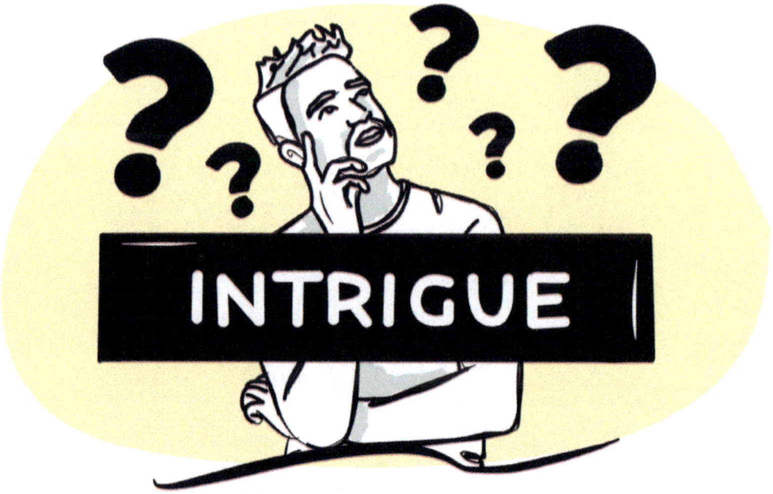
INTRIGUE

Let's Talk About the Fear and Failure

Fear and failure are two really dominant narratives when we talk about change. And they're probably the least helpful.

There is a lot of clickbait content out there, claiming that massive percentages of changes fail and that the biggest blockers to change is fear. Most of it comes from a good place, to warn you that change isn't always heaps of fun. But a lot of it is miss used or misguided. This is our take on it.

Let's start with failure.

Now I'm not sat here with my rose-tinted glasses on throwing ripped up petals across a wasteland of failed change. I know change doesn't go to plan. It doesn't because people are involved (and people are a pain in the arse). But getting hung up on out-of-date research from the best part of 15 years that was probably based on people and organisations that are nothing like you isn't going to get you far.

So, letting someone else's perceptions of failure cloud your judgement is really dangerous to the point of debilitating. Lots of consultancies lead with it to get you to buy, and when you've bought, you'll still fail because you didn't ever have the honest conversation about what success looks like. You never agreed what was good enough. Instead you have a pile of PowerPoint slides and a box of tissues to help you wipe away your tears.

In order to avoid being a failure statistic we want to know what your change will look like if its not absolute perfect. This next activity isn't a well-researched model or even science, but its 3 variations on perfect. Its 3 changes delivering 75% of the outcomes or progress. To some that's failure, but to most of us that's brilliant progress. Starting here is a great way to manage your expectations, in answering the above propositions you'll also know which one feels better and which one worse. So aim for the best 75% you can get your hands on and start there.

Using the prompts below describe your change as if these descriptions were true. Start with: How would they feel? What is at risk? What are you proud of?:

Your people are pushing back on the new world, but the change is progressing to plan	You deliver the most important things, and your people are at ease	Your people are adapting, but the core change is not where you need it to be

And when we talk about failure, it's pitched like some explosion with mass casualties. But most days it's a bit late, more expensive and not as impressive as we promised 'the board'. In order for you to make the best and most consistent decisions challenge yourself to know your tolerances and to be really transparent with them.

Some of the answers to the questions that follow, you should probably keep to yourself (because not everyone will like, understand or appreciate your answers), they'll be your own guide a bit of a moral compass (especially when you need to take a tough call, or if you have a wobble).

Take a few minutes to reflect on your current change, and consider where you stand on:

Your people: will you sacrifice them, upset them or mislead them to deliver?	
Cash: do you know how much you can invest and is there more if you need it?	
Outcomes: do you know your most important outcome and are you prepared to protect it?	
Time: is there a deadline or just a promise?	

And as for fear? We aren't that convinced it's a thing (or at least not *the* thing that you should be worrying about)

I don't need to know anything about your change, your organisation or how you are implementing it to tell you why its being met with grumbles. People will give you a hundred different reasons why they don't like what you are selling (listen to them – most of them are valid and will help improve your chances of success), underlying it all is uncertainty (which is nothing personal).

Human beings are hard wired to wobble during change, its our brains fault. Change equals uncertainty, and uncertainty equals danger. Danger makes us anxious and fearful. To keep us safe, our brains make up hundreds of unproven stories every day. And most of us go straight to the worst-case scenario, over-personalising threats, jumping to conclusions and underestimating our ability to handle any of it. It's primal.

We like to stick to the status quo (even if it's not the most efficient or effective way of doing things). Its familiar, its comfortable, its predictable.

Take a minute to cross your arms. Feels alright, right? That's because Its familiar, its comfortable, its predictable.

> ⚠️ **NOW TRY TO CROSS THEM THE OTHER WAY. YOU'RE EITHER GOING TO HAVE NO IDEA HOW TO DO IT, OR IT WILL FEEL WEIRD, UNCOMFORTABLE.**

But seriously, your brain will do almost anything to find certainty. Its less stressful to know you are going to miss your train than it is wondering whether you will or not. When you know something for certain, you can start to accommodate the outcome, whatever that is.

So, when you rock up with your great ideas to improve stuff, most people simply won't want to do it. Even when they agree that doing something differently might work better, actually doing it is sometimes just too much. And some will respond so negatively you'll wonder what the hell is wrong with them. Go easy – they are dealing with a whole lot more than just your proposal. This stuff runs deep, really deep.

What the hell do you do with all that?

You remember you are dealing with individual humans, it doesn't matter how many. And you acknowledge it. You acknowledge that this stuff feels uncomfortable. Sometimes it is very uncomfortable. There are questions. People are worried. And that's ok. What concerns can you alleviate immediately? What do you not have an answer for? And why? When will you know?

You meet people, you talk to them, you listen, you take on board what they say. You may need to adjust what you are doing, or when you are doing it, or how you are doing it.

Sounds too much like hard work? Too difficult? Too long a process? Then try implementing change without listening to people, without addressing their (very real) concerns or without responding to what people are telling you. It will be really difficult, if not impossible. And it will probably fail.

To protect your chances of success (and your mental health):

- Expect people to push back, welcome it if you can (this is where you find out what will really trip up your lovely project, not at the board meeting)
- Go to where the noise is (don't avoid it)
- Acknowledge this is uncomfortable (but don't be patronising, people aren't stupid) and be open about what you do and don't know
- Take time to listen (preferably face-to-face as much as possible, failing that try not to do it via bloody email)
- If the feedback is suggesting you might need to change course, or do something differently make the necessary adjustments or adaptations to what you are doing
- and tell people. Like a 'you said, we did' in a sports centre, demonstrate your listening and action

You also need to know that you cannot make the grumbles go away. You cannot make people better at coping with uncertainty – it's a mind-set change and that's not something you can change overnight. To make them more comfortable you can help them find the opportunities in the changes, you can help them focus on what they can control, and you can try to let your enthusiasm for the unknown rub off on them. But you can't do it for them. Accept it is part of the process and you are half-way there.

People don't actually fear change.

People worry and fret about the unknown parts of change, terrible ideas becoming a reality and even more so, crap implementation that leaves everyone feeling just a bit pissed. If your change is suffering because your people aren't on board, or they're sabotaging what you are doing (probably not in ways as dramatic as it sounds) you need to find out why

People derail change because:

- They disagree with the change, it might jar with their belief systems or expectations.
- The way you are going about it is making them feel unseen or disregarded, overwhelmed or overworked.
- They're directly and negatively impacted by the change.
- They have no idea what you're on about (most likely).

All of these things are ok. They're all human responses and they're all solvable. And not one of them has anything to do with fear.

Unfortunately fear comes with a narrative that it's the individual's fault, that they need to be coerced into change. If we break down the push back we get from our people, its often small and really bloody normal because as people, we simply don't like change;

- I'M BEING IGNORED
- I DON'T HAVE THE TIME & SPACE
- THIS ISN'T WHAT YOU PROMISED
- THIS CONTRADICTS WHAT I BELIEVE TO BE RIGHT
- MY ROLE ISN'T CLEAR
- I DON'T UNDERSTAND
- THIS IS DIFFERENT TO THE SLIDE DECK
- IT'S UNFAIR & INCONSISTENT

And the cause of these pain points aren't rooted in people are fearful of the change, it's that you aren't giving them what they need to make decisions, build understanding or make progress. **And that's on you.**

The Change in Hand

We have talked around your change quite a bit, so before you move on take the time to capture what is actually going on, what is changing? This will ground you in your change and will bring to life what you are up against. Completing this will help shape how you engage with the rest of this book, and will act as a reminder as to why you are here, feeling what you're feeling. It doesn't need to be perfect, it's for your eyes only.

WHAT IS CHANGING?

Recap

We are off. The book has officially started and your warm-up chapter is done. The foundations for what comes next are laid and its over to you to start to understand how what we will share can uplift your change and, hopefully uplift you. Because this book was written for you.

Key takeaways:

- It starts with you. And that can feel heavy, so understand why you might do what you do or feel how you do. Let that form part of your story and approach.

- Failure s a concept that we can overcome by being clear on your outcomes and expectations – more on that soon.

- Fear of change isn't real: fear is primal, the response change creates is closer to home, uneasy, lack of stability, uncertainty, lack of control a bit discombobulated. But nobody is running away from a tiger.

- Change leadership isn't for everyone and it doesn't need to be for you.

Action points:

If you haven't articulated your change, get on with that first. This will set you up for what comes next.

And if you didn't do it when the chance arose, pop back to page to the start of this chapter and take a moment to reflect on your relationship with change, this is your starting point and it might fill you with confidence or make you feel a bit wobbly. Either way, being mindful of your experiences and how they may make you feel, will help you navigate what comes next.

Problem 1) Is It the Right Change?

In this section, we are going to get under the hood of your change. If you don't have a change in hand at the minute, don't sweat, there's still plenty of value. The exercises that we have ahead of us are things that you can come back to. This section is super practical, we'll give you ways to get change clarity by establishing a clear understanding of what you are doing and why, approaches to communications, some ways that you might choose to measure your change and to just to keep you honest.

When we are done, you should have an idea as to whether you are comfortable with your change, with a clear line of sight to the outcomes you want.

When we talk about the 'right change' we are not talking about perfect change or outcomes. I would tell you any day of the week that change isn't perfect, no matter how much planning you do or what capability you invest in. and perfect shouldn't be your ambition.

Good change is what we are aspiring for here. Doesn't feel very fancy? Probably for the best. When you experience good change, you'll realise theres nothing average about it. It is fan-bloody-tastic.

And what do we know about good change? It will always need to adjust, adapt and change course. One day your change may even need to just stop. If we make every decision based on where we are, what we know (and I mean actual evidence, not just your gut) and what your people can cope with, then your change will most probably be the right one.

And that change may need to adapt its course, but it won't implode.

Here we go.

Types of Change

There are only two types of change: planned and unplanned. That's it. Only two types.

Planned change tends to be when an organisation is proactive about change, seeking it out, horizon scanning, linked direct to evidence and strategic intent. Planned change by its very nature makes the road a lot smoother, establishing or deploying change early.

Unplanned changes are often reactionary, to a problem or an opportunity. We didn't see it coming, we weren't ready. And now it is here and wow! Reactive and unplanned change tends to happen in organisations that are 'too busy to change' and find themselves deploying changes to mitigate issues that ambush them and seem to scramble after opportunities they identify late in the game.

Think about your change. Where do you land?

Planned and unplanned change create two very different change environments. Planned, by its very nature often comes with a level of order and control, it comes with better viability of what you are up against and what the road ahead looks like. For the sake of a good chapter (and a casual insinuation that you might have bought this book because you're knee deep, or expect to be soon, in some unplanned change), we are going to focus on how we tackle unplanned change, and the feelings and experiences of chaos that often come with it.

Dealing with chaos, is about getting some stability as soon as possible. You cannot deliver in chaos. No, not even you.

And here's how we are going to do it:

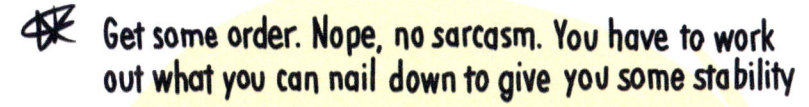

- ✶ Get some order. Nope, no sarcasm. You have to work out what you can nail down to give you some stability

- ✶ Be critical about the change. Does it really need to happen now? If not, stop. It won't help anyone. If yes, what is the minimum you need to do to solve where you are?

- ✶ Create time to really understand what needs to happen after your minimum solution is in place. And start to shape that in a planned way.

- ✶ Establish the core of your change in a way that is planned, controlled and as un-chaotic as possible.

Change thrives under a bit of pressure, we all do. But it doesn't thrive when the ground is moving, the sands are shifting and everything feels like…chaos. So, pop your superhero cape back on the coat hook and take 5 minutes to identify what one thing you can do within your change that will calm a little bit of the chaos:

CALM THE CHAOS

and as for transformations, don't get me started.

If you're reading this book and I got my pitch right, it's unlikely that you'll be punting for a transformation. Because the goal of transformation is to reinvent the organisation. It needs such more than your average change. And probably more help than a book you bought for a tenner. Why split hairs?

Let me explain. Change, or the process of change management is focused on implementing finite initiatives, which may or may not cut across the organisation. The focus is on executing a well-defined shift in the way things work. It's not easy, but we can handle it because the core of your organisation remains the same, or at least relatively stable.

Transformation is another animal altogether. It is a cacophony of initiatives which are related, cross cutting and possibly undermining of each other. Its job isn't to shift, it's to reinvent and transform your world. Its more unpredictable, iterative, and experimental. It will come with a high risk and high reward, so you'll need an iron gut to take one on, where total failure is a very real outcome.

But there is still a desire to transform, a weird need to declare a transformation or transformative journey. Made worse, by prefixing it with Agile, Digital or Organisational in the hope that it will feel fancier or deliver better. And then, my personal favourite is when we name them. Dropping in a quirky name won't make it more relatable, or accessible. Neither will a logo (even if it will look great on the launch day cupcakes). If you're reading this and you're feeling the transformation vibe, I want to challenge you because I reckon, if you're honest and out of the eyes of a board or exec, what you're up against might be a whopping change, but it's not a transformation.

Not convinced? Reflect on your change and see if you can articulate the:

- **Scale of the change based on the impact to colleagues or customers (scale of small to massive)**
- **Whether its planned (a good time before you opened this book) or un-planned? (scale of planned to unplanned)**
- **Is your organisation change order or chaos? (order to chaos)**

If you've answered massive, planned and order, I'll let you call it a transformation (if only to move on) but if you've answered massive, unplanned, chaos, my advice is to hit the brakes now. And anything in between - read on.

Change Clarity

We might need to change. We might have to change. Perhaps we should change. We might simply want to change.

Clarity during change is the *best thing to have*. It's also essential if you want to bring people with you and the linchpin for delivering well. And it's pretty easy to get it.

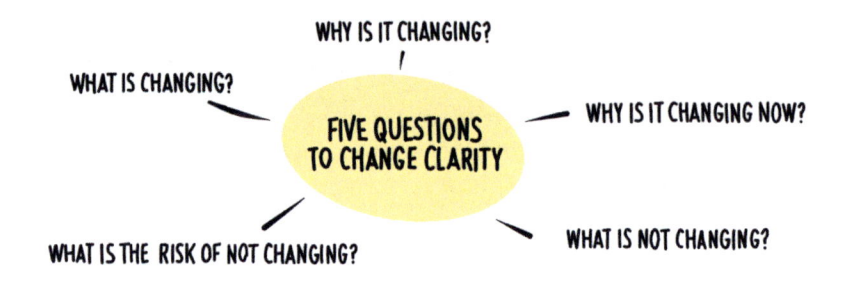

FIVE QUESTIONS TO CHANGE CLARITY
- WHY IS IT CHANGING?
- WHAT IS CHANGING?
- WHY IS IT CHANGING NOW?
- WHAT IS THE RISK OF NOT CHANGING?
- WHAT IS NOT CHANGING?

Articulating your change challenge away from strategy documents, big presentations and flouncy exciting postcard statements is where the money's at (and sorry if you're reading this after you have crafted the *most perfect* change ambition and printed it all over promotional postcards). Why? Because in the clear light of day, when there's not a board that needs to be appeased or seduced, it just comes down to you and the change in hand. In order to rise to the challenge ahead, you need clarity on what you are doing and why you are doing it. With this, you can have a clear line of sight that things are going the way you need to get you to where you're heading. Without it, you're not going to get very far, or have a lot of fun.

Take a bit of time to answer each question now. It doesn't need to be perfect, it's only for your eyes (do it in pencil if you have to).

WHAT IS CHANGING?

WHY ARE YOU CHANGING?

WHAT IS STAYING THE SAME?

WHAT IS THE RISK OF NOT CHANGING?

WHY NOW?

Your ability to answer these questions means you can articulate the heart of your change away from the flounce. The core of your change is here in five little boxes. Use this as your change compass to help your make decisions, tackle problems and build confidence. This is what you are here to lead.

Refer back to it, and don't do anything that contradicts it, and the day you aren't able to do that, stop (reset, review, or actually stop).

Is it the Right Change?

The journey to right change isn't mine to give you. Only you will ever know if the change is right, but there are some incredible tools to help you get there. A personal favourite is establishing a Theory of Change. It's a single take on why a particular change can deliver the ambitions or needs of your organisation. It shows how change happens in the short, medium and long term to achieve the intended impact (and I love a bit of change impact). It's also a great visual and brilliant for bringing people together to co-create and talk about.

A theory of change gets you to work through:

YOUR PROBLEM   YOUR CONTEXT   KEY STRATEGIC DRIVERS   ASSUMPTIONS   SHORT TERM GOALS   MEDIUM TERM GOALS   LONG TERM GOALS

The right place for a Theory of Change to be created is at the start of your change or strategy, you can use it to describe something that is in progress but for us, trying to establish whether your change is right, the best place to do it is at the beginning.

> **HERE ARE SOME GUIDELINES FOR HOW YOU SHOULD GO ABOUT COMPLETING ONE, WITH A TEMPLATE READY FOR YOU AT THE BACK TO GIVE IT A GO**

The most important thing to remember is a Theory of Change has to be real. You shouldn't over inflate, or skim over key impacts. You need to have an idea of activities, events or action you need to take so you know what you are signing up to and so you know the journey that you're committing too. Where possible you should be looking to:

- Use previous insight to support its development, that might be 'proper' research or from your stakeholders.

- Do it with what you have. There's no change team at the end of a Theory of Change and as I said at the start, it's likely that as a change leader with this book in your hand you have to work with what you have, not with what you hope for.

- Co-create it with your people, defining, drafting and shaping your Theory of Change to the point where you have general agreement that it feels right and feels achievable.

- Give as much detail as you can for your outcomes, you want them so they can be tracked, tested or measured. Doesn't need a dashboard, but they need to be identifiable.

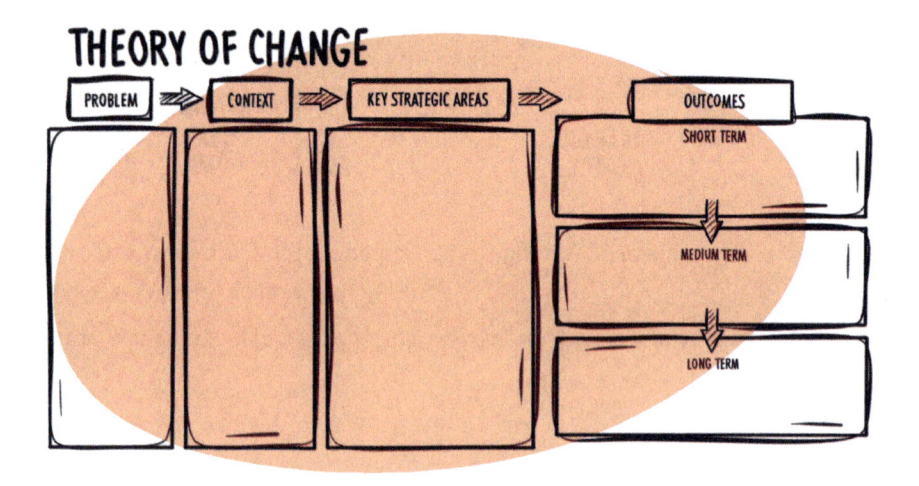

THEORY OF CHANGE

PROBLEM ⇒ CONTEXT ⇒ KEY STRATEGIC AREAS ⇒ OUTCOMES

SHORT TERM

MEDIUM TERM

LONG TERM

If you can complete a Theory of Change, your change will be grounded in reality, understood by those who create with measurable outcomes. It can't tell you if its right, but it will give you indicators to spot if it might not be delivering the outcomes you hoped, and give you the opportunity for course correction. Defining your change this way increases its likelihood to be the thing you need because of the work you have done to get here.

Change Goal Mapping

Now we know how the changes look in terms of strategic intent, assumptions and outcomes. Now it's time to talk about what that means to your people, processes and products and what you might need to do about it. We're going to establish your change goal and lay the foundations for the journey you're heading off on. This activity and outcome is your softer more in-tune change journey that will enable your people to recognise when the change is working well, or not quite hitting the mark all without needing a grand reveal, a new widget or implosion.

> **NOTE: WE ARE BUILDING ON THE OUTLINE OF YOU CHANGE CREATED IN THE LAST CHAPTER, IF YOU HAVEN'T DONE THAT OR ARE STARTING FROM ANOTHER SPOT, YOU'LL NEED TO ESTABLISH SOME CONTEXT IN ORDER TO GET THE BEST OUT OF THIS**

The best place to start is, as ever, by bringing your people together to have this conversation. Through this conversation I want you to talk about what the world will be as you travel through your change (this might be time boxed or it be based on what you can deliver). Your conversations should focus on:

- What the outcomes might mean to individuals and teams?
- What will they create or stop?
- What might they open up?

These three components will generate the conversation that help you articulate your change goal. It's purposefully not an objective because objectives tend to be a little bit…boring (and your strategy should give you one of those, right?).

The reason for us using a goal is to be something to aim for. Something big and challenging. It's not something to tick off a list. You want to make it as big and ambitious as you can, cram it with beautiful adjectives and verbs. Make it feel triumphant. Take five minutes to see if you can articulate a goal for your change:

ARTICULATE A GOAL FOR YOUR CHANGE

Now I know, not all goals will end up on the sexy goal spectrum making our bellies feel fizzy at the thought of it, but even so, make it something to aim for, to act as a catalyst for the changes ahead.

And when you have your goal, its time to map your journey. This is the hearts and minds bit, less about the delivery and more about the feels. We're going to be creating a map to help you guide the change based on how the change feels. We are doing it this way because your spidey senses are better than any data in an excel spreadsheet. It will also be super visual whether held online or pinned to a wall, it's the guiding hand for you and your people.

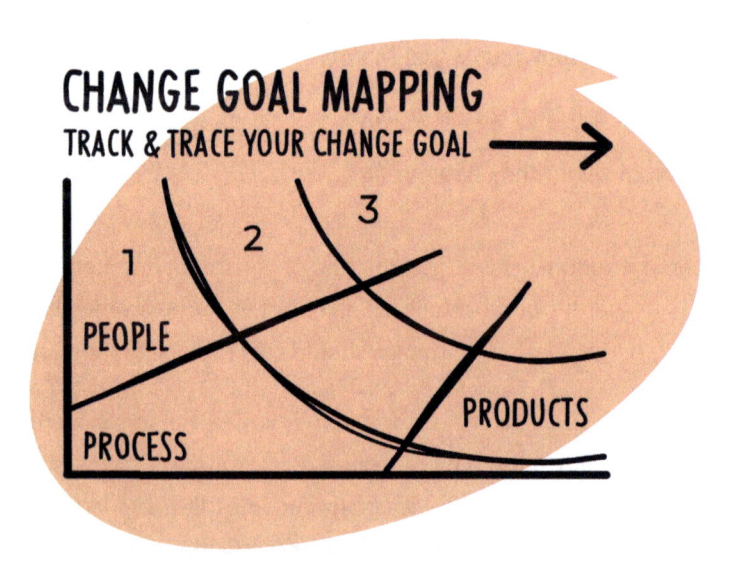

CHANGE GOAL MAPPING
TRACK & TRACE YOUR CHANGE GOAL →

1 2 3
PEOPLE
PROCESS
PRODUCTS

When you map your journey, you're going to want:

1. A handful of timeboxes between where you are now and your change goal. These will sit at the top of your change map.

2. To know what's in scope of the change, it doesn't have to be everything but try and chunk together what you do (e.g. into products, processes or services) and you should aim to include everyone, these areas will sit around the edges. And you're looking for about 3-4 areas to focus on.

N.B: if your organisation is pretty massive, or your people are better split out into slightly nuanced groupings then the advice here is to not try and get it on one page (but 10/10 for trying), but to have multiple maps (centred around teams, services etc.) that all all working toward the same goal.

To complete you map consider for each timebox and for each area:

- **How might it feel?**
- **What might be different?**
- **What might we lose, or need to let go?**
- **What we might need to know?**

What should it look like? The answer here is the terrible, *it depends*.

If you're going through structural changes and your people will be given new roles or expectations, your first timebox is likely to reflect lots of questions, feelings of unease, a bit disruptive. But the timebox closest to your change goal, I'd hope the description felt brighter, more at easy, learning new ways, feeling supported, adjusting to new routines. However if you are launching a new product and the people impact is minimal, or 'later' your first timebox might be more focussed on awareness building and as you get closer to your change goal the focus shifting towards confident use, or the ability to sell.

The point is that you articulate a shared journey, one that can be recognised by people affected and understood by everyone else.

Through asking (and answering) these questions we can start to articulate how the change may be felt. so, grab the sticky notes and get going.

I want to describe each moment in time in this way so when we are moving through our journey, and it starts to feel 'off', you'll have something to call it out, something to tell you whether you expected it to feel rough or if something is adrift. It's a great way for your people to recognise this too and to help by raising early warnings or help with course correction.

Measure What Matters

Who doesn't love a KPI? Ha! I feel you. An old boss of mine use to say it stood for the quickest way to Kill Performance, Innit. This isn't a lesson in those. But when we head off face first into a change it's good to know if what we are doing is going to get us to the right place, so knowing what that might look like is really helpful. You have started to pull some of these together in the outcomes you will have identified and in most cases these will be enough, especially if you have been able to quantify an outcome or have a line in the sand that you're working toward (or away from). If you haven't then this is probably worth a read.

> **THIS ISN'T A LESSON IN STATISTICS BUT A QUICK LOOK AT OKRs (OBJECTIVES KEY RESULTS) AND BENEFIT REALISATION**

OKRs

'OKRs' stands for Objectives and Key Results. At the time of writing this OKRs had got a bit trendy, but they had existed in back corridors of creative organisations for yonks. Depending on how they are used (like any tool), they can be massively helpful. But OKRs do need a bit of discipline. If your organisation already uses them, then it's an easy win to apply them to your change and be able to talk about it in a language or model that folk already understand.

For clarity, they're not just fancy KPIs (Key Performance Indicators). They start with an objective that's actually akin to your change goal. They should feel ambitious, so their starting point is slightly different. They aren't the same as the objectives that we set our people and teams, the ones we write on a form and them file away for 12 months. These objectives are your lighthouses, north stars - call them what you want - they are the thing out there in the distance that you are trying to get too. And the key results will tell you if you are creating progress and impact, if what you are doing is working, or more importantly not working.

So, an objective is big, ambitious, action-oriented and real. A key result is specific, time-bound, helpful and measurable.

Because we are going to use the key results to guide our change, it's important that we talk about how to achieve big goals, track progress, and get measurable results. This isn't a job you do sat in your office. It's something that you can do as part of your Theory of Change, or Change Goal Map. When you create them, you're initiating a pattern of review (this can be to any pattern that suits you and your change) steps 1 & 2 you'll do once, and then you'll do steps 3,4 and 5 in a loop to keep you honest and your change moving forward.

One	Two	Three	Four	Five
Co-create them with those responsible or impacted by the change	Set them and stop messing with them	Share them to get some accountability	Review progress looking for any warning signs that things are adrift	Adjust activity to improve key results (as needed)

The Mythical World of Benefit Realisation

Benefit realisation is often forgotten (or just plain old ignored) when we get the agreement to change. But its where the money is (both literally and metaphorically) when it comes to change. There's always a risk that we progress something without knowing what we are getting. Some of that you will have addressed in your Theory of Change when you identified some of the details around outcomes.

A big challenge with benefits is that we can over-complicate it or shoot for the moon and fall short of even getting the rocket in the air. If we write our benefits with the wrong evidence or for the wrong audience.

So, our approach is very much around finding the joy, making it meaningful and being proud. Because we know when you can see opportunity, when you understand 'what's in it for me' change becomes easier.

We structure our benefits in a way that utilises the sum of its parts.

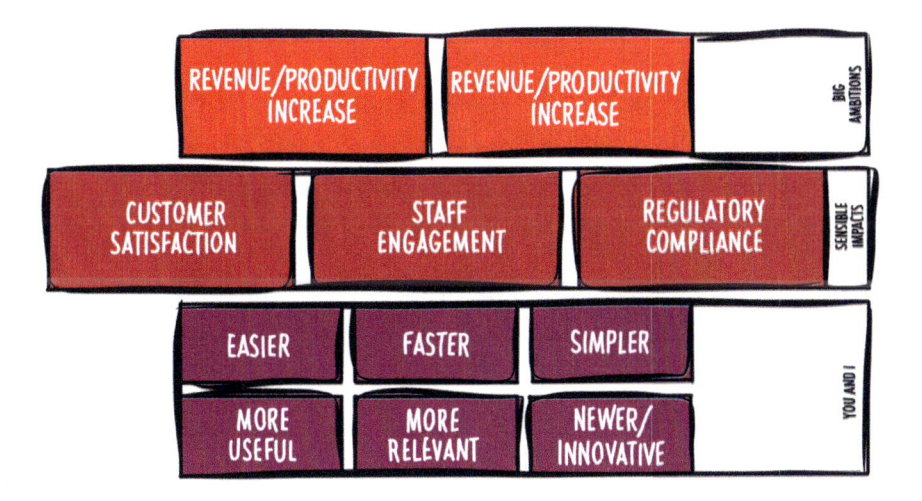

REVENUE/PRODUCTIVITY INCREASE	REVENUE/PRODUCTIVITY INCREASE	BIG AMBITIONS
CUSTOMER SATISFACTION	STAFF ENGAGEMENT	REGULATORY COMPLIANCE	SENSIBLE IMPACTS
EASIER / MORE USEFUL	FASTER / MORE RELEVANT	SIMPLER / NEWER/INNOVATIVE	YOU AND I

Big Ambitions: these should be the benefits of your change goal, be big and ambitious and you only want a couple. These are your lighthouses in the storm, you may never really get to realise them fully, but they are the catalyst and driver behind what you do. If you can even get close to achieving these, you have done a smashing job.

Sensible impacts: these are the normal things such as improved outcomes, or increased sales. They're the things you would hope to achieve and be able to measure. These are likely to be aligned to your products, processes or services from your change goal map, you want a handful. They can be linked to your KPIs but they should not be your KPIs. Its like knowing the triple 18 on dartboard is better than a bullseye. These are your value creators.

You and I: the best benefits. These are the improvements and nudges that you and your people will see. Everyone should have one (or two). These are how you know you are delivering for each person, their benefit might be linked to the outcome, the change process, or getting to spend more time with different people. 100% personal. You can do this anonymously, but I'd opt for building some trust and knowing what benefits your people are looking for.

Is it Right?

If you can work through this chapter and do your best to answer or complete the activities, be open to making adjustments to your plans, course or action and outcomes, then it's probably as good or as right as it will get.

So, asking if it's right, is probably not the question you want answering, I expect you're somewhere wondering; will they like it, will they do it, will it work, will you mess it up?

And the answer is, probably.

Because in every change event, you get the rough with the smooth. Day's when you're winning followed by a slap around the chops you didn't see coming. I often describe a core change skill set as 'being able to roll with the punches' because it's not hearts and flowers all the time, no matter how 'right' you get it. It can't be. Humans aren't made that way. And you know what. It's ok.

It is perfectly fine to know that parts of your change will create discomfort, frustration, push back etc. It's not ok to pretend that won't happen. So, we tread a fine line of understanding that what we are doing may cause a negative impact, wanting to get it right and not holding yourself over a barrel. And the gap between getting this right and feeling like it has gone horribly wrong is under your control - from the actionable steps you take to get it right and how you feel about how others feel.

One of the biggest lessons, that it took a bit too long for me to learn, is you aren't responsible for how other people feel and how they react to what they're hearing or seeing. That's not yours, its theirs. Ergo you are in control of how you respond to their reactions. This is something you'll only learn to manage through doing, there's no short cut or model to nail this one.

(!) BUT THE LESSON HERE IS RESPOND, DON'T REACT

Recap

Is it the right change? Was the problem we set out to solve. With the chapter all about giving you some practical ways to identify and pressure test your change to make sure your change is right, with a clear line of sight to the outcomes you want. And as you'll now know, the answer to this question will always be 'it depends'. Which I know is (and I am comfortable with it being) an absolute cop out. Because how 'right' your change is, is bound by your context and your people, exactly the way it should be.

So, whilst the answer will always vary, the approach won't. Getting started in the right way is crucial. Preparing for any big event whether it's a big birthday, wedding, marathon or this change, is instantly easier by getting the foundations right. And by that we mean making sure you know what you are doing, why you are doing it and what you want to get out of it.

Key takeaways

- Know your reasons for changing and have clarity that is real and repeatable.
- Understand what is good enough and be absolutely proud when you get there.
- Measure what matters; find a handful of indicators that can help you know when you're winning and give you a clue when you aren't.
- How 'right' your change is will be determined by your people.
- Change is personal and so is how people feel. You aren't responsible for how people feel.

Actions

Get on with identifying your benefits. It's a really quick and simple task that will help you work out whether it's all worth it. There will be something in there for you, your people and your organisation that will make what happens next easier and more pusposeful.

PARTICIPATION

Problem 2) You Don't Actually Know What You're Doing

Hold on to your tiny horses. You do know what you're doing.

The last chapter focussed on getting the change right and now we need to do something about, in the best possible way. And when we say best, we aren't talking platinum coated, multiple certifications and a trophy type 'best', but best in a way that uses what you have and delivers a change that you can be proud of, that's our kind of best.

When you start a change, it can feel a bit cliff-edgy. Because you don't know what's going to happen and because when our primitive brain dominates, we instantly opt for fight or flight options only…and some days it's easier to just leg it.

This chapter is all about identifying mechanisms, tools, and ideas to support you by working out an approach that works for you, your people and your change. Because change is personal. We'll be looking at how to co-create your Change on a Page, so it's all in one place. And for those of you who just want to do something, we've got a bit of a shortcut to getting things moving (disclaimer: the shortcut only works if you have done your homework and you know your change *really* well). We'll introduce some really simple planning techniques so you can track key activities, explore how you can get the right people around your change and then really understand what happens during a change as we transition from one world to the next (not a weird time travel thing).

So What Now?

You know your change, you understand the outcomes you are looking for and have the path laid out. So next step, a complicated change strategy? Nope, wrong. There's always lots of fancy chat about having a change strategy with an idle threat that you'll need one to get anything done. And that may be the case if you're a mega-corp and you're transforming a transnational business (if this is you, hint: you probably need more than this book), but until then we'll start with getting your change on to a single page. These little beauties are brilliant. You don't need anything fancy, some clear space or a wall and some sticky notes is smashing.

The purpose of this job is to answer the most important questions you and your people will have when your change is introduced. It builds on the work you have already done, so you're not starting with a blank piece of paper but creating a visual that gives you the chance to bring your people together to shape the journey ahead. And you can bring *lots* of people together, which opens up your change to become part of your organisation.

The best way is to co-create it, through a facilitated session using sticky notes on a wall (because you can't have a workshop without a sticky note, eh?). And purpose behind this as an approach and an activity is all about getting your people to open to up to where you are, where you are heading and what it will mean for them. It's not to convince or seduce, it's there to build a shared understanding.

You'll be working through:

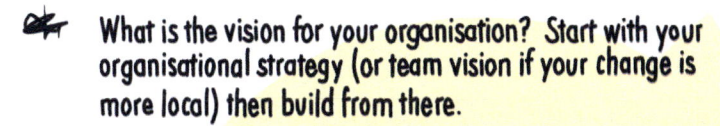

- What is the vision for your organisation? Start with your organisational strategy (or team vision if your change is more local) then build from there.
- Why is this change important to the organisation? Explore the change, what is its role within the organisation and how will it help get you closer to that vision.
- How will you measure success? You can have this as an open conversation or you can use outcomes, benefits or OKRs you have already thought through and open them up for challenge, definition or adjustment.
- What does good look, sound and feel like? Your change goal map will be really helpful here to bring together all aspects of the change.
- How will we show progress? These are the indicators that show your organisation is heading in the right direction.
- Who is affected by the change and what will they need to do differently? This is an early impact assessment, where we are understanding the relationship between your change and your people.
- How will we support people through the transition? What do they need to be able to respond to the change?
- What's the plan? Early identification of what may need to happen and when.

Out the back of this brilliant conversation, you'll be able to capture your Change on a Page (give or take) which will guide your delivery. My only caveat being it's not about what is on the actual page, it is, as ever about the conversations. So even if you can't answer all the questions, the fact you're asking them is smashing and you may need to re-visit them as your change evolves. And I encourage you to re-visit them as often as you can, or as often as adds value to what you're doing.

Our template gives you an example layout that you can use for your final version. For your workshop session you can just figuratively carve up a wall, use an online collaboration tool or split the work across tables. At the back of the book there's a bit more practical advice as to how to use it.

CHANGE-ON-A-PAGE

VISION

WHAT WILL GOOD LOOK LIKE?	HOW WILL WE KNOW WE ARE GETTING THERE?
WHO IS IMPACTED?	WHAT IS IMPACTED?

HOW WILL WE SUPPORT THE CHANGE?

WHAT WILL HAPPEN?

NOW	NEXT	LATER

Kan-do Kanban

There are loads of ways to plan and schedule your work during change, but it's hard to not try and do it all at once. If you start everything it will all get finished, right? Realistically the more you start the less you progress. The challenge with multi-tasking or stacking up priorities is you stop being able to see the wood for the trees and you end up with *so much* work moving, it blocks itself and you end up with delays and conflicts just because you let too much stuff run ahead.

We're going look at using Kanban (a Japanese word for visualise), specifically a Kanban board, which started out in lean manufacturing and is now a staple in agile project management. Core to its design is the ability to help see your work and see it flows from to-do, to done. It helps you limit work-in-progress because you can see it moving through, or not, and it enables teams to commit to the right amount of work (rather than chasing dates on a plan) and get it done.

There are 3 main things you need to get your Kanban working for you and your team:

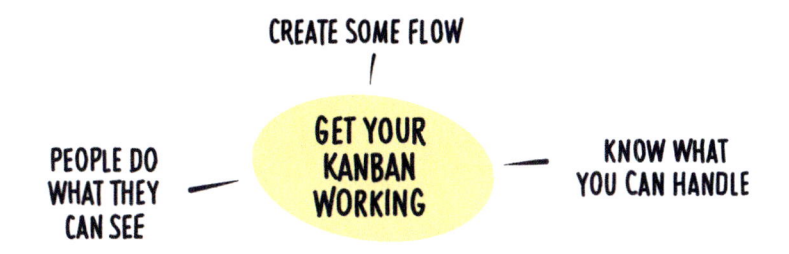

```
                    CREATE SOME FLOW
                           |
                    GET YOUR
    PEOPLE DO    —   KANBAN    —   KNOW WHAT
    WHAT THEY         WORKING       YOU CAN HANDLE
    CAN SEE
```

People do what they can see — the entire point is that you can see your work i.e. all activities are captured. This can be on virtual tickets, stickies, cards or something more creative (but probably not the back of a fag packet). You'll write all of the known work onto cards, one per card. If helpful, you might want to link the activity to part of the change, so that the context travels with you.

Now you have them, get them on to your board, this is now your world and it will help teammates and stakeholders quickly understand what the team is working on.

Create some flow — and we do this initially by using columns, I know sexy. But very practical and crucial. Each column represents a specific activity that when you look at them end-to-end it gives you a "workflow". Cards flow through the workflow until completion. They can be as simple as "To Do," "In Progress," "Complete".

The *To Do* column is the home of ALL of your work. *In progress* is where the stuff you are working on sits and *complete*, well that's the stuff that's done. You might want to have: a column for 'blocked' if your organisation is likely to throw a few spanners in the works, or if you have some heavy governance to navigate. And 'wish list' of all the lovely things you'd like to do. Emphasis on the 'like and lovely' because you can only do them if you make great progress or get more resource, so they stay on the wish list until then (consider yourself told).

Know what you can handle — or for those more au fait with Agile ways of working, we are talking about work in progress (WIP) limits. This is the maximum work you can get to any one time, and in this case they are a maximum number of cards that can be in one column at any given time. It's the estimated amount of work that you can get through (warning: you will over-estimate, but remember it is better to under promise and over deliver).

It's unlikely that the first time you use it you can guess the right amount, so my suggestion would be to start with three per column (beyond the to-do column). For example, a column with a WIP limit of three cannot have more than three cards in it. When the column hits three, or has pressure to squeeze in something else, the team needs to view those cards and move them forward before new cards can move into that stage of the workflow.

WIP limits are critical for exposing bottlenecks in the workflow and they also give you an early warning sign that you committed to too much work. Review the WIP limit as often as you need, but don't try and just 'do more' you'll end up doing less, and badly.

The Right People

Change is all about people.

A key contributor to successful change is having the right people wrapped around and underpinning your change. This isn't about stakeholder management; this is about the able and the willing.

THE ABLE AND WILLING

A different look at the traditional 'change agents' and; change resistors

Ability
- Understanding of the business area affected by the change
- Understanding of the change being proposed or progressed
- Knowledge or skill to help move the change on

Willingness
- How willing they are to support your change
- How they can help bring people with you
- How much support they can offer you

	LOW Willingness	HIGH Willingness
HIGH Ability	Able to identify opportunities for change, but not act on them	Able and willing to establish the new world
LOW Ability	Unlikely to be willing or able to move the change forward	Can generate enthusiasm and motivation but won't have a holistic view of the change

Let's talk about those who'll help you and your change succeed. We call these the 'willing'.

They are willing because they like the proposed change or they may want to try to fix the same thing you want to fix. They are usually firm believers that the paradigm of 'we are where we are' is naff, and that we should be aiming to get to places that are better. This is glorious, blinking marvellous and single-handedly creates a bright dynamic within a change of getting up, getting started and getting the change over the line. It is the best thing for everyone.

Quick to follow we have the 'able'.

These are the folks with the skills or knowledge you really need, subject matter experts, those with high levels of authority (informal or formal) and they often have a bit of a 'following'. They have a wealth of knowledge, ideas and ability and it's likely that they'll get you places, unlocking the next level in your change so you can build momentum, design solutions that actually work and deliver your change in a way that can be understood and received. You need them.

When you have started to identify these folk, what you'll start to realise is that this might feel like a relatively small group, or small in comparison to what you thought you'd get.

WHAT DO YOU DO NOW YOU HAVE THEM?
PUT. THEM. TO. WORK.

The reason you want these people in your change is to get them to do some of the heavy lifting to help manage the change impact that you are creating.

These two groups can exist in isolation, they can contribute to your change from their respective corners and they will still have a positive impact on what you are doing and the experiences of those around you. But imagine how good it could be if you brought the together? If you created a synergy that enabled these folk to work together, to underpin your change from a point of belief, capability, and reach. You don't have to do this in a way that is contrived, you can create communities that bring these individuals together and you can just ask for their help. Both work. Both add value. Both will make your change better.

Those who you haven't identified as willing and able haven't done anything wrong (and for your next change they might just be the people you are looking for) and it's really unlikely that you'll find any malice, but do expect to uncover the odd few that are just sodding awkward. Some are apathetic, but some are doing cooler stuff than you. They aren't your people for this change and it's really fine. Your gut will probably suggest you should be begging and pleading to encourage them to join a formidable force of 'willing and able', but my advice is to move on, let them be. Continue to share your ideas in ways that are accessible, be clear on the implications they might experience, and be open to their questioning and challenge (it might just make your change better). *But stop burning time on them.*

Change Isn't a Solo Sport.

One of the biggest lessons I ever learnt was that you do not need to do this stuff on your own. Sometimes you feel like you are on your own with this stuff, especially when you are the one leading the change. It can be damn lonely. You are not alone though, there are others who are dealing with the same stuff. There are individuals or small groups of people (not necessarily just those directly involved in your problem, but with bags of empathy) dotted all over.

Yeah, you can see and hear the wave of people who might be against your change all too loudly. Its always easier to hear the criticism of dissent, as humans we are just glutons for punishment.

But there will be another group, a quieter group, who are not only supportive, but can be your greatest allies. They are quiet right now because they get shouted down, they feel like they are on their own, and they've been labelled as trouble makers. These are the people who see the issues that need changing and raise their head above the parapet to point them out or suggest what could be done about it. They often get told: no, sit down, don't rock the boat, stop being disruptive. The phrase they hear most often is "we tried that before and it didn't work". After a while this gets pretty miserable and they either leave or give up. Neither is a good outcome.

The able and willing are your people. These are the people that will help push change through.

> **FIND THEM, HELP THEM FIND EACH OTHER, GIVE THEM A PLATFORM AND SPACE TO FIND THEIR VOICE, THEN LISTEN.**

Done well, this is powerful stuff - this is how you can start to change how your organisations thinks and responds, dare we say it, it's how you can change your culture (whoa-there cowboy, that's a whole book in itself!). But for now, create a community for them, with them.

I'm not talking about the kind of communities that meet to spout bullshit to each other about how successful their most recent project was, when everyone knows if you scratch the surface you'll find out they are using a hell of a lot of poetic license when they call it "successful".

I mean the groups where people are honest, open and supportive. They get to the nitty gritty, sharing their issues honestly, collaborating to find solutions, really supporting each other in trying to make things better.

These communities can help build trust and collaboration where previously there was suspicion and division. They can improve the knowledge and skills of an entire group of staff just through the sharing of the existing experience within the organisation without any need for additional investment. And even if individuals aren't getting support within their own team directly, they find confidence and empathy within the group, all of a sudden its not a lone voice, it's a movement.

Do not underestimate the power of human connection. Here's how to get started:

GET THEM TOGETHER

FIND THEM — GETTING STARTED WITH THE POWER OF HUMAN CONNECTION — **LET THEM TALK**

- **Find them** – start with your team or those directly involved in making your change happen, then open it up for anyone who has a voice they want to be heard. There will be voices all over the place.

- **Get them together** – ideally in person at an event. Making connections is one of the most powerful aspects of this. You don't need everyone all at once, so take what you can get and build it from there. If you build it, they will come.

- **Let them talk** - let them compare their battle wounds and war stories (a good moan does us all good, and helps us bond a bit too). They will realise that they are not alone, other people are in similar positions and this will empower them.

Then start to build on what you have:

HELP THEM FIND SOLUTIONS TOGETHER

CREATE A SAFE SPACE FOR THEM — **THEN START TO BUILD WITH WHAT YOU HAVE** — **KEEP THEM FOCUSSED**

- **Create a safe space for them** – you need to build trust and that means you are going to have to be brave and share some of your own challenges. If you can find a couple of others to do the same, then even better. Be honest, don't sugar coat it.

- **Help them find solutions together** - find out what keeps them up at night and respond directly. There will be similarities so you'll be able to identify topics. Solutions might come from advice from an external expert, someone internal sharing how they did it, or the group might work out their own solution between themselves.

- **Keep them focussed** – make sure the themes or topics discussed directly relate to the issues they are facing. Allowing them to get things off their chests is fine, but the idea is to find answers to problems, not just talk about them.

Enable them to see the change they are creating;

USE THEM TO SPREAD THE WORD — **ENABLE THEM TO SEE THE CHANGE** — **PALN FOR THE LONG TERM**

- **Use them to spread the word** – they will become your Heineken (reaching the parts of the organisation you wouldn't normally) and as well as bringing issues or concerns to the group, they can take messages back to their respective areas as well.

- **Plan for the long term** – this lot can help the whole organisation get better at change long term, by helping their own teams understand the world they are moving in to. But they'll also need to be able to see their path and influence in action, so don't keep them under a bushel.

There isn't a precedent in terms of size, you don't need three hundred and eight people, donuts and matching t-shirts. You need time, space and opinion, I expect there's plenty of that on offer.

Communities can feel a bit sweetness and light, something for later, when there is time.

BUT HEED THIS WARNING; DO NOT UNDERESTIMATE THE POWER OF COMMUNITY DURING CHANGE

You have an underutilised (and underestimated) workforce that just needs some space and someone to listen. There is strength in a group of like-minded people, especially when things get tough (and they will get tough) these are your people, let them be there for you.

Step Off the River Bank

In order to change, you need to move, to transition. And to do something new, something has to end, which might seem paradoxical but it's true. Bridges Transition Model is all about your people and their experiences of change, how they move through it and what they may come across and experience. It's less rigid than other change models (ahem) and enables people to occupy multiple spaces. More importantly it allows your people to actively participate in their transition and gives you ways to provide tailored and scalable support. It is all about you and them.

It's formed around three phases; the Ending, the Neutral Zone and the Beginning.

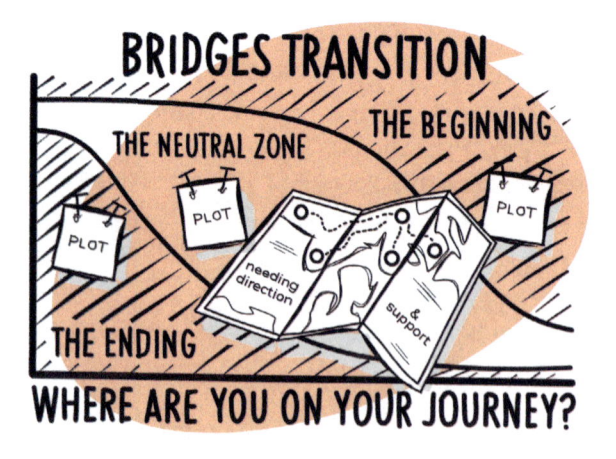

BRIDGES TRANSITION
THE NEUTRAL ZONE — THE BEGINNING — THE ENDING
WHERE ARE YOU ON YOUR JOURNEY?

Endings. When a change begins, something has to end. Endings signal the literal end of the current state. People have to let go of how things were, and they also have to let go of how they were or used to be. Some of the things they might need to leave behind include relationships, team members, processes, etc. it doesn't need to be sad, the emotional response doesn't need to be prescribed. In fact there doesn't need to be one, some people may just be ok. This is like standing on a riverbank and looking across the river to the other side. Endings is the start of new ways and new worlds. It's that first foot off the riverbank and into the water below.

As you and your people understand and accept the journey ahead remember you are heading there with a plan, you know what is ahead of you (in the main). Use your plan to enable early quick wins to demonstrate progress and build momentum, removing barriers and blockers quickly as they appear to keep everyone moving onward.

Neutral Zone. In this stage, people have accepted that the old way has ended and are starting to understand what's ahead of them and what they need to do. There is a risk here, that in the Neutral Zone it can feel a bit 'eugh', and we refer to it as the sticky middle, where your people can literally get stuck as they lack direction or enthusiasm to do differently.

This can be where your change starts to come unstuck, where your people can't find a way forward because the path forward isn't clear and the outcomes uncertain. At this point you have stepped off the riverbank and you are waist deep in cold water and you need help to get out of the water, so send in the metaphorical life jackets and give your people something to hold onto that can move them onwards.

Despite the challenges of the Neutral Zone, this is also the time where your people create, explore and try new ways of working, so it can also be a time of innovation and experimentation, so get the guard rails in place to enable them to be creative and generate their own progress.

New Beginnings. If the Neutral Zone is handled with care and your people are given a chance to be curious and creative, you will start seeing how people become active participants in the change rather than simply being subject to change. When this happens, they are transitioning to the New Beginning phase. Where the new world isn't something to be feared but is an opportunity to start doing differently and start feeling the benefits. You'll see people climbing out of the river, helping their mates to do so too and looking back to those who need a bit more help. This is the start of change stability. As soon as new beginnings come into sight, celebrate. And shift your focus onto creating a culture of consistency around new ways of working and the importance of their role in the new world.

So, what do you do with it? For me it's another great collaboration tool, that helps your people find their place in the change and seek the help they need to progress. Using on online collaboration tool or a white board you can create the three phases of transitions and ask your team to plot where they are and (if helpful) how they feel, what they need or maybe a question they have.

By doing this, you start to bring your change to life, sign posting to problems and opportunities. You have the chance to see:

- where your team is and maybe understand some of the behaviours you may be experiencing. It can also give you the chance to provide some clarity through the questions you might be posed.

- if there is a problem; a prolonged period of people in the neutral zone could highlight that your people don't have enough to move forward with and that something needs to happen to avoid your change stalling.

- when the majority of those affected are settling into the new way it will help you spot any stragglers who might need a helping hand to get out of the other side.

Working through Bridges as a team activity, or a temperature check can create a safe space to surface unease, provide clarity and comfort, which during change is a wonderful thing to be able to experience. It will also give your people the chance to understand who might be feeling the same as them, or someone who could help them progress or get answers.

You can also use it for you, as an individual activity, because knowing where you are is as important as knowing where everyone else is.

Talk About It

"Change is just comms and training": said nobody who is actually serious about delivering change, ever. But we can't just gloss over the fact that comms is crucial to getting this right. And remember we're talking to three different parts of the brain, not just the faces staring back at you.

Regardless of whether the upcoming change is positive or negative, it pretty much always leads people to react emotionally (even if that response is apathy). And from experience (and probably some clever research and science) when bad news comes out of the blue, we tend to see it as even worse than it actually is.

So, we're going to try and do it in a structured way.

This isn't a template change strategy, but as a leader of change here are 5 things you need to know:

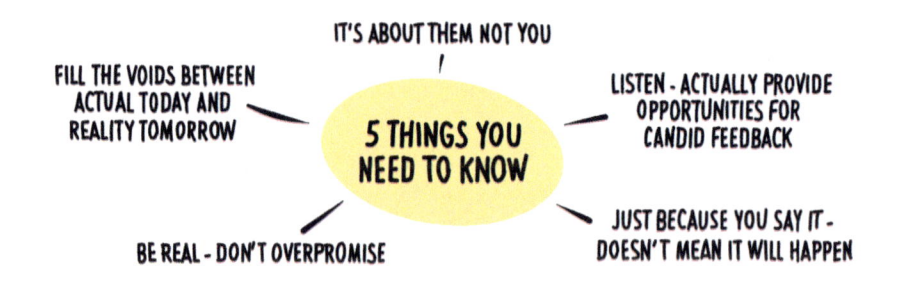

5 THINGS YOU NEED TO KNOW

- IT'S ABOUT THEM NOT YOU
- FILL THE VOIDS BETWEEN ACTUAL TODAY AND REALITY TOMORROW
- LISTEN - ACTUALLY PROVIDE OPPORTUNITIES FOR CANDID FEEDBACK
- BE REAL - DON'T OVERPROMISE
- JUST BECAUSE YOU SAY IT - DOESN'T MEAN IT WILL HAPPEN

What can you do about it?

1. **Be real - and don't over promise**. Inflated statements turn people off and lead to mistrust of the entire message. And it will catch you out, big time. Whatever you say, your people have the right to hold you to account over it.

1. **Fill the voids**. When change happens, it leaves a void between what is actual today and the potential reality of tomorrow. People will fill that void with whatever they think the new reality will be. Try to fill that void before it is created, even if the filler is 'no news today'.

2. **It is about them - not you**. Unfortunately, when something is hard to communicate, it is easier to talk about yourself or use the language you are accustomed with using. I see this a lot with procurement - we use our jargon, our benefits, when we should be using our organisational language and communicating what is in it for them. This happens a lot during heavy people change; where a line manager might start a hard conversation with 'this is really hard for me' and that might be true but imagine how it must feel to be the receiver.

3. **Listen - actually provide opportunities for candid feedback.** Seek it. Large meetings. One-to-ones. Surveys. Forums. Think of almost every way someone would be comfortable communicating back with you about the change and enact it. And what we have gone through so far gives you loads of opportunities to bring folk together. At the end of the day, change doesn't happen with your door closed, so open it up to everyone.

4. **Just because you say it - doesn't mean it will happen.** The "I say so, so it is" leadership days are gone. People have to have the desire to change. If you tell them to change, you will create a reactive culture and you're likely to trigger the primitive brain.

Constructing comms needn't be a mine field, there's a really simple structure that we work with that re-caps, re-enforces and re-sets.

1. **What did you say last time?** Not a total recap, but something that can ground people in the change context e.g. last time we were together I shared/we spoke about X.

2. **What do you need them to understand?** What are the key takeaways? Outline them at the start, cover them in the middle and re-cap as part of your close.

3. **What do you need them to do?** This can be a simple as; to listen and to ask questions or a request to sign up to training or join a workshop session. Be specific about the action include time, dates and methods.

4. **What happens next?** After comms, one of the first questions is often "so what next"? If you know the next steps, share them. If you don't, say that you don't e.g. "what happens next will be dependent on the outcome of the workshop I have asked you to sign up to".

5. **What do they need?** Outline the support or opportunities that are available, open to questions and be comfortable with a bit of silence. A great

technique is to share something you want them to hear or be reassured about in disguise as a question asked outside of the room, or after the last session e.g. "I received a question after the last session and I thought it would be helpful to share the answer with everyone…or a prompt that provides some clarity e.g. "after the last workshop I was challenged on my assumptions on X, this is what I shared…"

And we want to see this structure in everything. It might take the fun out of impromptu comms (which should be as controlled as possible!) but it will get your people used to how you are talking about the change, reinforce key message and provide stability.

How you deliver it is up to you. Delivery is always unique to the person delivering it, but I would suggest some experimentation and definitely doubling up on your techniques.

Human to human comms: always a great way to demonstrate confidence in your change and to treat people like they're real and not just statistics. But not everyone can be there, so set up a video link for people to join remotely and record the session, get support to facilitate questions. But get it in the diary in advance – nothing screams danger than a last-minute urgent face-to-face meeting.

Email: For me, should always be for a follow up, or a "no new news" message. Landing something super important on an email will set you up for it to be missed. Email is your second command e.g. so you may have to deliver 5 face-to-face meetings where you'll focus on progress and intermediate updates, real dialogue on what you are doing, but you'll share of outputs to those in the room, or those who missed it on email. But PLEASE do not send a bad news email on a Froday, no matter how 'known' it is. Just don't.

Let Me Tell You a Story

Storytelling is as old as time. We have been sharing stories since before we could speak with symbols and finger painting on cave walls. It's probably the earliest form of teaching - keeping our history, knowledge and experiences alive. Stories connect us, across time as well as space. The stories we tell shape how we see our world.

Stories communicate facts, but maybe more importantly, they convey emotions. And that's the crux of it when it comes to storytelling and change. Because no one ever changed for a strategy. We don't do things differently for a vision statement. And we definitely don't make things better because the project plan said to!

If you really want people to change, you have to get them emotionally. And if you think that's rubbish, that it's impossible to get someone to be emotional about the implementation of a new IT system, try implementing one.

Humans are driven by emotion (cheers brain). We like to think we are logical (and we can be) but when things get tough, we get emotional. And change is tough. I'm not saying everyone will start sobbing into their tea at the launch event, but people will respond emotionally when you start to change things. We can't help it. We are hardwired this way.

Good storytellers can use that emotion, combine it with facts, throw in some embellishment and boom! They've suddenly got a whole room full of people laughing/crying/calling out for a new IT system…well, you get my drift.

> **TO CHANGE THE NARRATIVE, CHANGE THE STORIES.**
> **THE ORGANISATIONAL STORIES, THE TEAM STORIES, THE INDIVIDUAL STORIES.**

Instead of the story about how the organisation takes ages to do anything differently, like that time they tried to change the way we processed orders back in 2010 and it failed miserably because people didn't like it and Jeff in Accounting told them it wouldn't work, but no one would listen and they did it anyway (shaking heads and pursed lips)…stop telling that story.

Start telling the story about how the events team spotted how they could make the process faster if they just took out that bit of unnecessary bureaucracy and saved the organisation time and money, and how it was rolled out across the country and they all got a bonus and two of the team got promoted – you know Sandra the Director of Operations? Yeah, she was part of that team and look at her now (raised eyebrows and a knowing slow nod).

Neither are 100% true. Neither focus on the little details. It doesn't matter. They set the scene for all that follows. They change the narrative of your change.

Our stories are our culture. We change the stories, we change the culture (there is definitely another book there…definitely). We change the culture to one that is more supportive, open and tolerant of change. We make it much more likely that any changes and improvements will be successful.

It takes time. It's not something you are going to do overnight. And I'm sorry, but a few finger paintings on the wall of meeting room 1 just aren't going to cut it.

You are going to have put your big pants on and tell some stories of your own. Preferably stories with some adversaries that were overcome, some elements of failure, but made up of (mostly) truths and triumph. Find others who have these stories (use your community). And start telling them and getting others to tell them. Because that's how you change the narrative, with a new one.

Tips for good storytelling:

- Choose an appropriate occasion - consider the interests of your audience
- Practice first - a good story has a beginning, middle, and end. The best stories build up suspense to a climax, and include some humour
- Start strong - capture their attention
- Ensure events are in the correct order so it's easier for people to remember
- Create believable characters - use real people and names where you can
- Engage people on an emotional level by sharing universal emotions that resonate with them (especially if it relates to something they are going through right now, and especially if you share those emotions)
- If you can, relate the point of the story directly back to the issue on the table - and how the story helps find a solution
- Keep your story short, but don't leave out the important bits

And like most stories, it doesn't have to be 100% true, but it does have to be mostly true and no literal lying. You were not chased by a bear and we aren't bailing you out of prison.

Do Something, Anything

I promised you a cheat. This is it. And arguably its not even a cheat. It's my 3 favourite jobs when executing a change. Whether you think you're ready or not, this is how to get out of the starting blocks and to get moving.

Job One: Do anything.

The hardest part (before the people get involved) is actually starting. Because then everyone knows and can see your change. The pressure you put on yourself will outweigh the pressure from others. It's like walking up to the mic for your first song on karaoke.

> **IF YOU DON'T DO SOMETHING, YOU, YOUR PLAN AND YOUR GRAND IDEAS ARE, WELL, JUST IDEAS (AND PROBABLY A LOT OF FAFFING)**

So when I say do anything, that's what I mean. Do anything. Because you do not know what you are up against until you start to move, take action and begin seeing how people respond. Feels dangerously reactive, you'll be caught on the hoof, it won't be polished? Maybe.

But it will feel worse if you've spent months telling yourselves that you are right and your ideas will be smashing and now you find out that, well, they might not be. And if they aren't you'll find out soon enough and that feedback will make your change be the brilliant thing you need it to be.

So do anything, I'm not asking for you to take a sledge hammer to a wall, book the first conversation, canvas some ideas, open your change up to those affected. Run a change canvas workshop, establish a Kanban. Make a move to make your change real.

Job Two: Load the sled

Yes, bobsleigh fans, the next job is to get your change on the way down the run. Not a bobsleigh fan? Don't worry, just keep reading.

Now we've spent time getting the change out in the open, signalling the new world or new ways, we need to get ready to iron out the kinks in our ideas and approach.

The best way to do this is to identify the people that will underpin your change – the able and the willing we discussed before. Start to bring people along, be clear on responsibilities, set expectations and get everyone ready to go.

It's now that people begin to learn and unlearn, shape their new habits, and resistance is likely. But rather than managing the resistance away, I want you to give it the time and space to make the change better by inviting it in, listening to what you are being told and deciding on whether you want to do something about it

The most important thing about Job 2 is to not rush. Keep planning, seek feedback, seek advice (seek the best advice you can afford, is what my Mam would tell you). Keep iterating, be open to people and ideas, break rules, make mistakes, but keep your anchor in your change. The guide for the run you are in – follow it, push it, test it, but always keep it in sight.

This phase still takes focus and attention and the natural frustration that comes with a learning curve will ask you to think and do differently. But you are running, and the sled is moving. It gets easier from here.

Job Three: Pace Setting

Establishing momentum is where it gets really fun. This is when your change takes on a life of its own. This is where we balance the pace you need and the pace of the change, because now your change has legs and it's having an impact. New habits are forming, the actions that used to be difficult become easier, and the change effort ceases to exist.

So now your organisation is working in the way you need. Your new world has its own pace, and it needs time to embed, to normalise, to find a sustainable pace, a drum beat that means the change stays intact and your people a part of it. Pace setting isn't about dates and timelines, its more about the cadence that you create, how messages are reinforced, how new ways are introduced and how you continue to earn until the change is done (and that doesn't often correspond to 'the date' on 'the plan').

> **!** SO, WHEN YOU PLAN THE PACE, REMEMBER YOU'RE SIGNING UP TO A MARATHON, NOT A QUICK DART ACROSS THE ROAD TO THE CO-OP.

Pace setting is a skill in itself, and the need for someone to have eyes on the pace could far outlive your change plans. Be mindful of this, bring it into the conversations that happen with your people and organisation so it stays alive, or at least it enables you to pass the baton on. You may need to do a full business cycle to really see the change stop being a 'thing' and to start being part of your tapestry.

Recap

You don't actually know what you're doing. This chapter was in part to show you how to do some of the things you need and part to remind you that everything else you are already capable of. Having spent time understanding your change we needed to make sure you went about it in the right way. So, one more time: you absolutely do know what you are doing, but it's completely normal to have a wobble, need some support or to have a solid whinge that everything feels shit.

Your ability to bring together your change clarity with the actual journey ahead is crucial and doing so in a way that doesn't drown your people is crucial. Because your ability to deliver great outcomes will come down to your people and if they are at 100% capacity with delivery activities, you will get deliverables, but you'll miss out on innovation, creativity, owned and sustainable change. Because these things don't happen "on the side" and they don't happen by forced collaboration. Use what we are sharing with you to enable time to think, be creative, learn and grow to establish change that's truly sustainable.

And you can always ask for help. It won't hurt you, nobody will laugh and you might feel better.

Takeaways

- Stay close to your why and keep change clarity in your mind, you lose this and you lose your change

- The most important thing about getting started, is doing something

- Don't over commit – doing more might feel great and purposeful. But if you really want to win, do less to do it better

- Communications will not be the thing that makes your change succeed, but it will be the thing that if its done badly will make your change come unstuck really quickly

- You were not chased by a bear.

Actions

Reflect on your last comms, whether it was about the change you're handling or something else but use the structure that we have just shared to help with a re-draft. How does it read? And more importantly how does it make you feel about the message you are landing?

REFLECT ON YOUR LAST CHANGE

Problem 3) There's too Much Stuff Moving and Changing (Everything is Urgent and Things Are on Fire)

Change is complex, but it's not complicated. And no, they're not the same thing. When we talk about complex, we're talking about multiple moving parts or multiple changes either linked or cumulative. Complicated, is when we make it difficult or convoluted. We do it, not by design or intent, but because the very nature of change triggers some primal behaviours in you, and the people that will wrap around you. There's a need for need for dates, the priority is 'great optics' and you're stood in front of lots of people; you might have gotten yourself in a pickle and your ability to deliver well is under threat or up the swanny.

This section is all about finding the simplest routes to the best outcomes. After all, we're not here to make it harder than it needs to be. When it comes to change *it's not what you do, it's the way that you do it*. This section will explore easier ways to get better results.

Step Away From the Big Bang.

There is often a desire in change to try and deliver it All. At. Once. Or in one big bang. Because when we do that, we get the launch day balloons and cakes. Whilst this is an admirable goal, it's tough and often thankless. More often than not it's a bit square peg in a round hole. With the final push being as many people as possible pretending that everything's how it should be. Its often referred to as *Big Bang* which is less like a firework and more like an organisational nightmare.

Big Bang can be a lot for you and your people to handle all at once and it can trigger a pretty whopping push back, even when you think everyone is ready. Because when the change is theoretical it can be rationalised or resolved. When it's real, well, it's real and that's likely to create a few WTF responses. Even in the most beautifully managed change, people will wobble. Whilst you don't have to disregard Big Bang, in some cases it will be needed and in some organisations, it might actually flourish, but for the sake of this book and the intent to simplify what you are doing and make it easier to navigate we'll be talking you off the Big Bang ledge and we'll give you three other options:

TO AVOID BIG BANG
- HAVE PERIODS OF STABILITY
- DO LESS
- HAVE SMALLER BURSTS OF CHANGE

Periods of stability. I am a big fan of periods of stability during lots of change as they are super healthy; they allow a change to embed and for the next phase of change to be created based on what has gone before. The risk with this approach is people will remember what you told them at the start. As your change embeds, the likelihood that you may need to undo or revisit something that's just been done increases or you'll be hit by cries of "but that's not what you said". This isn't an insurmountable approach, but needs care and stability in terms of organisational structure. It works better if your change is to maximise an opportunity rather than respond to a risk or problem.

Doing less. A valid option, yes, but it is often really hard because your change is there for a reason. This will put pressure on your ability to prioritise what you are doing across your organisation or within the change. This splits out into two options, the first doing less across your organisation, with some work being stopped, paused or re-shaped. The second; you could identify the minimum you need to achieve and focus on that. This requires A LOT of discipline because you'll need to define the minimum, stick to it and manage the expectations of those wanting or needing more than what is on offer. This is always one to consider, but not one to lose sleep over.

Smaller bursts of change. This is where we have lots of incremental changes that have a cumulative impact. Change is delivered to the organisation in smaller "chunks" over time, where on their own their impact is a bit 'meh', but collectively they realise a much bigger 'ooooh' response, with less drama and likely more control. whilst you might not be able to deliver the end product or solution to your people in chunks, as a leader of change, you can absolutely deliver this in a more incremental manner.

Smaller bursts of change is our go to in terms of delivery. And naturally we think you should start here as well.

This is how we do it:

1. **Look for opportunities to engage your people** in early discussions about what's ahead, this might be demos, workshops and playbacks. Do this early and often. Don't worry about showing an unfinished solution or idea, be clear about where you are and build on it.

2. **Co-creation** is not just a management buzzword, it's a really beautiful thing. Create time and space for your people to be involved at every opportunity to co-create - not just the solution, but the change approach itself. A brilliant visual way to do this is with your Change on a Page (which we covered earlier), as it enables your people to come together to shape, test and understand what is being created and why.

3. **Timebox.** A change that runs 'forever' is miserable. By time boxing your change, you are creating moments in time where your effort results in value. It's when you get to showcase, show off and have a little rest. It also means those people who aren't directly involved in your change can see what's been happening, understand what it means for them and demonstrate progress in the journey you're making.

Progress Over Perfection

Part of the heavy load during change comes from the stories you will tell yourself and the weight of that expectation can feel heavy.

It's a lovely pattern of thoughts that will ticker tape past our eyes during any period of 'big decision'. As leaders, in any capacity, we tell ourselves that we have to come up with the answer. There is an expectation that on the day you are affirmed as a leader you get issued with a whole lot of sass and the ability to provide single, definitive, correct and perfect answers. And that my dear, is heavy and wholly untrue.

Looking back on our neuroscience lesson, we know that our brains are braced and raring to go when it comes to claiming uncertainty as a risk or threat. This is especially true for those of us responsible for leading and landing change - we are surrounded by people, especially boards and committees that are looking at us to define and deliver the "right" change. This is both daunting and a bit bloody annoying. And it adds to the complex world of change that we are actively trying to solve.

As we try to address it, it's likely that we'll unleash another leadership pit of despair aka the 'I might as well do it myself'. We are now trying to solve two problems, the need to get it right and the desire to do it all. Which I can confirm is bonkers. Take the time to understand where you can best help, create progress or unblock the path for others. When you've done this, and put your superhero cape away for the day, try and release something (anything) to the people around you, who I expect are all pretty capable and smashing (if only you'd give them a look in).

So, Let it Go

Perfection is futile, useless, boring and definitely thankless.

Perfectionism is rooted in our assumptions of everyone else's expectations. I feel like someone else wrote that. It feels a bit profound to drop it in mid-page. I think it's true. We create something that isn't real and we pursue it and we work at it to sort it, respond to it and erase it. However, it was never there in the first place.

Progress is where the money is. Progress gives you the ability to move and the space to make mistakes and to learn. Now it's easy for me to say, when it comes to delivering change. I have made lots of mistakes but I haven't made the same one twice. That's learning in action.

If you can identify what is needed to move you forward, if you can define and agree what good looks like and start taking steps toward it, you have progress. And everything else? Take the time to loosen your grip and let everything else go.

Start by writing a list of what you can control and what you can't. For what you can control, write down what good looks and feels like to you and your people. Use that to keep you honest. Oh, and put what you can't control on a sticky note 'over there' until its status changes.

WHAT I CAN & CAN'T CONTROL...

Look Out on the Dance Floor

I'm a great fan of breaking changes into their smallest components. From a delivery perspective you have a better command of the work in hand. It enables changes to land with a greater ease than a whopping big lump. It can pull you, as the person responsible for the change, into the weeds and then you start actually doing it, and that's one to watch out for.

I expect if you're reading this book, you might have a bit of a bias for action and become pretty frustrated when you can't get the job done. As a change leader, you need to balance your need for action with preparing and supporting the world the change is happening in.

Knowing the nth degree of your change but losing sight of your strategy will cause you bother. Spending too much time working through niggles in a plan rather than supporting organisational engagement will limit your ability to get traction and make the impact you need. Standing in the middle of the dancefloor watching every ones moves, will not make people want to dance with you.

So, whilst you will desire the dance floor because it will feel safe and homely, and the thrill to be where the action is, will be appealing, you need to be able to keep your total organisation in sight and have a more holistic perspective to give you the chance of delivering the change you need in a way that you can be proud of. This isn't me telling you to sit in the metaphorical cloakroom whilst everyone is having a great time, but a caution that getting too involved, doing rather than leading will mean your ability to see red flags, enact course correction or see opportunities will be hampered (and your people might find you a bit annoying).

It's time to spend more time stood at the bar watching the dance floor than advising on the dance routine under the disco ball.

But yes, if you're asking, I'm dancing.

Culture Eats More Than Strategy for Breakfast

You might wonder why this is in the complicated aisle. It's here because culture is both complex and complicated. A double whammy. Culture is the dominant narrative in our organisations, it tells us (whether we recognise it or always agree with it) how an organisation works, what keeps it together, what makes it what it is. Some are fancy (and maybe slightly forced) with big wall graphics and matching pens. Some are the outcome of doing what we do in the way that works for us. Others are disjointed and emergent. But whatever state your culture is in, it can derail or just gobble up your change.

For change to have any chance of finding its legs and making progress it needs to contribute to, support or build upon the culture of your organisation. If your change turns up trying to take a sledge hammer to your culture or take another culture out on a date it is not going to end well. Your prevailing culture will feel threatened and it will become defensive. Your culture will call her mates and they'll take on your change without hesitation. It's like when your best mate starts seeing someone new, everyone needs to get on to make it work. When your change is likely to butt up against or want to influence your culture be mindful that for some people this will be imposing and jarring, it will go against their very being so the response is not likely to be joyful.

Be open if your change contradicts values or behaviours and share the why. Be open if your change will actively disrupt the culture. And make time to listen.

Quick caveat: you can't and shouldn't change your culture each time you introduce change, just because what you do is changing, who you are and why you do what you do, is probably the same. And realistically, you shouldn't have to launch a change in order to change your culture. You don't sheep dip your people in a new culture and you can't just cut the old one off; but you can work with it in the best way.

What do we need to do then? Start with your outcomes (you know the ones you wrote down at the start) and the narrative you built through your change goal map and then:

1. **Understand if behaviours need to change to get to those outcomes (direct or indirect), focussing on how people need to participate or engage for the change to succeed.**

2. **Actively find the barriers to that behaviour change - where do they exist, do you have access to them, where do networks and followership fit, do you understand the culture landscape your change is navigating?**

3. **What can you do to move or address the barriers? What or who do you need to do this with you or for you?**

By working through your change and its impact through the lens of culture, we can create a path with enough space for the culture and change to co-exist or pass peacefully.

Doesn't mean you have to like your mates' new date though.

4 Boxes

Most of us will have dabbled in the Eisenhower matrix at some point, it's a really simple tool to help you sort out your life without a massive to-do list. If you haven't come across it, it is centred on setting priorities based on the importance and urgency of the stuff you need to tackle. The important ones are those that lead us to fulfil the established goals and the urgent ones are those that can have undesired repercussions if they are not performed in a timely manner.

> **IT WILL HIGHLIGHT YOUR PRIORITIES, STUFF YOU CAN DELEGATE, AND THINGS THAT CAN GET IN THE BIN!**

We use a variation on this for understanding your change(s) and your organisational landscape, because your change does not operate in isolation, it is crashing against other priorities and competing for the same resources. Like in business, it's really important to know your competition.

And this competition extends from changes and resources into business-as-usual activities, often all under the pressure to do less with more and still have smashing outcomes. We often find ourselves squashed between what we need to do, what we want to do and what we should be doing. That can feel messy - a bit chicken and egg in terms of what to do for the best. It makes working out what to change, and when to start, really bloody hard because there's a little voice at the back of our head that thinks it will be easier to just live with the problem, accept the risk or let the opportunity slide, than take on the effort to actually make the change. It's a similar problem to delegation, where we tell ourselves it's easier to live with a short term problem by 'doing it yourself' than initiate a change in how you work by bringing someone in on what you're doing. It's not something we talk about, but we both know it's true, right?

But whilst we are deciding that we'll 'change that later' there are to-do lists popping up everywhere from strategies, meetings and chats in the kitchen. We create work and that can feel daunting, especially if you need to know where to start. The best thing to do is get it all out on the table and remember where we are and where we want to go. This is a great way to empty your brain, but also to bring your people into the conversation, to talk about the world you can create together; you can start from your strategy or just a good chat about your business plans. From this point we can start to identify your change landscape and what you're up against.

And here we take the Eisenhower matrix and make it more 'changy'. This approach will help you do some early work to understand what you're up against and where you need to focus. It's a quick and dirty way of separating the stuff that will happen (because its part of who you are as an organisation), where you might need a tactical intervention and when you might need to create and prioritise a change activity.

	STRATEGIC	TACTICAL/BAU
OPPORTUNITY		
PROBLEM		

This process will help you take a worry list and translate it into something you can action. It will also help you see that not all priorities are equal. Call them whatever you need, but there is a distinct difference between a fundamental change of organisation purpose and sorting the annoying admin thing. Use this as the chance to understand what is happening around you, and to choose what you need to do (and what you don't).

Capability and Capacity

Too much change is a beast. It makes delivering change harder and the experience literally miserable. Knowing when enough is enough isn't as easy as a spreadsheet. There's literally no instant formula or fix for knowing how much is too much (or more scientifically, when you'll hit change saturation). It is absolutely unique to your organisation and people. When one changes expect your capacity to change too.

What actually is it? Without labouring the point, it's the volume of change you can cope with aka your change capacity. With limited capacity, there is only so much change you can handle, it's like squeezing into a pair of jeans that are a size too small – there will be resistance, overflow and general feelings of discomfort. When you exceed that capacity changes will feel rough, your people a bit naff and your changes won't be as effective as you need.

There are loads of factors that can influence your capacity to change.

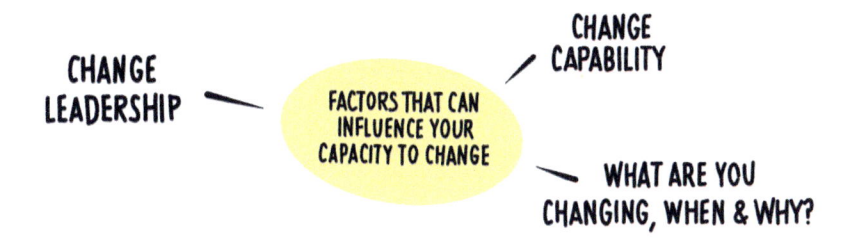

CHANGE LEADERSHIP — **FACTORS THAT CAN INFLUENCE YOUR CAPACITY TO CHANGE** — **CHANGE CAPABILITY** — **WHAT ARE YOU CHANGING, WHEN & WHY?**

1. **Change leadership:** as leaders you will have a massive influence on your organisation (we are focussing on the great aspects of this, not the bits that are slightly daunting) ergo change leadership is a significant part of how change is managed and delivered. Effective change leadership can build on the capability of teams to be more agile and capable of absorbing more changes. Effective change leadership can also help to maximise how optimally the change is socialised and implemented and, therefore, how it lands.

2. **Change capability:** do your people know what to do? How to actually

change? How to challenge and how to ask for what they need? If the answer to any of these is no then your capability needs some work. Without some foundational capability for engaging with change push back. This will be the first response limiting your capacity (This isn't a bad thing. If change is new to your people and organisation you're much better off doing one thing well than six things badly. It will also grow your change muscle so you can change more/better/different in the future).

3. **What you are changing, when and why**: maybe I should have led with this one. Realistically, one of the biggest problems is that your people do not know what is going on in your organisation. Combine an unknown expectation with a busy-as-usual day job, and your capacity to change is instantly under pressure.

So how do you get a handle on your capacity?

1. **Find some indicators**. Whether it is person by person or a team level, identify a handful of indicators that can tell you what's going on and I mean indicators that can be consistent measures (not something that changes like the weather). These are important because during change (and more importantly when we start to hit saturation) you're likely to see it in your chosen indicators.

2. **Listen to your people**. Feels like an obvious thing to say, yeah? Unfortunately, when we have indicators/KPIs etc. to help us, we can rely on them too much and stay committed to the data. At which point you lose the drum beat of your organisation – what your people are thinking and feeling. Change saturation is often in capacity to 'do' but it's also hidden in capacity to think, focus and switch off, and you won't find this in a dashboard. Regular conversations will help you spot trends and call out bias.

3. **Know your organisations patterns and peaks**. Every organisation has a routine, where activity is at a peak, or where we choose to protect a certain time of year. If this is the case, the likelihood of implementing a change then, successfully anyway, is probably unlikely. So, know where

they are, what they mean and how you can avoid them or mitigate the impact.

Recap

There's too much stuff moving and changing. Well, tell me something I didn't already know I hear you cry. We are asked to change all the time, whether that's stuff moving aisle in the bloody supermarket, or more significant changes in our organisations. And to be honest some days it's hard to keep your shit together. This chapter set out to try and calm these waters.

And we've covered a lot. Some of this will play directly into what you do. Most of this will be about how you feel. This book is yours, it's a handful of pages that are here to help you, feel more equipped, able and supported. To help you feel more confident by taking perfection off the table your change is already closer to you than you think. Having a structure to communicate we take away the complexity and give you sustainable consistency. By helping you see the wood for the trees, you can make better decisions or, at least, informed decisions. Change can feel complicated, messy, urgent and unnecessary. You are told this (repeatedly) because drama sells. But it doesn't have to be your reality.

Takeaways

1. People need to hear what you are saying 3-5 times because they actually hear what they are being told. Consistent simple messaging is your friend

2. You cannot do it all. Choose where to play, if you want to win. Let everything else stop or slow.

3. Perfection is shit.

4. You need both the capability and capacity to deliver well. Having loads of people who do not know what they are doing is as damaging as having three people do all the work.

5. You can mention discos in a business book.

Take Action

Look at your change in its current form, if you had to break it down into three components (it can be more than three if it makes sense, but a minimum of three please!), how would you do it?

Now look at it again, and break it down again, looking for at least 2 smaller packages of work for every "big" one.

```
[COMPONENT 1.]   [COMPONENT 2.]   [COMPONENT 3.]
  /    \          /    \           /    \
[ ]    [ ]      [ ]    [ ]       [ ]    [ ]
```

Focussing on the smaller packages of work, reflect on how you can deliver them and what your first move would be?

WHAT'S YOUR FIRST MOVE?

Feels like it could work? Crack on then.

Things You Need to Know About That Nobody Talks About

This book is intended to be a completely honest opinion of change with some helpful stuff to get you delivering, but there will also be things that nobody talks about, or nobody discusses in public, because views are a bit polar, there's not enough (if any) research, etc.

And some days it will feel like the world and your change is just happening to you, that you aren't good enough (bloody Imposter Syndrome) or the person stood in front of you is so convinced they are right we don't know which way to turn. So, we don't talk about the stuff we are worrying about, or what we disagree with in case anyone rumbles us. This section is to crash out a few myths, or to try and answer the questions or assumptions we know some of you are thinking about.

You Don't Need to Do it on Your Own

Despite this book being designed to set you off on your way and that change leadership is sold as a solo adventure, I am an advocate that you should buy the best advice you can afford. I'm not writing this as a consultant, I am writing this because I spent years trying to sort it all out myself, do the change, be the change and teach the people. It is exhausting and really inefficient. Conveniently there are people out there that know it, have lived it and want to help.

When you start on your change, work out what you need by looking in three different lenses; you, your people and your organisation. This will help you to understand what you can afford to lose and what you can afford to do, and start to balance what you can to make the change work (and more importantly to work with what you have).

- You don't need to get your whole office writing strategy and dissecting your data, but there will be value in investing time in a workshop to explore the change ahead where the data will be really crucial.

- If your secret ambition is to have everyone certified and earing matching t-shirts, I'd start by investing in a coach to help you navigate the tricky points.

- Agree the tools, techniques and language that you want to use and doing so with a bit of advice and support from someone who knows how would be great.

This isn't me, trying to flog you consultancy, it's me trying to help you understand where you might need back up. We know that time, money or people doesn't grow on tree's and when you have a back drop of change competing for your time or that of your people it's hard to make the call as to where to play or where to spend. So you can self-assess the help you might need using the below 5 questions using 1-5 scale (5 being the most positive and 1 the most naff).

Litmus Test	You	Your People
1. Do you understand the change as explained?		
2. Do you feel confident in talking to colleagues about how change may impact you, them and our organisation?		
3. Do you feel you have the capacity to respond to the change in the way it has been explained?		
4. Do you feel that your line manager can provide you with the support you need during the changes ahead?		
5. Do you feel you have the capability to respond to the change in the way it has been explained?		

Crib notes: Here's how you might respond to any low scores you've hit for the five questions

1. You need to get a consistent message out, if you have big team or or-

ganisation then comms support might be helpful, exploring videos rather than emails could give you better reach.

2. This one could be helped by facilitated action learning sets, mentoring and coaching.

3. Treat low scores as red flags, indicators that you need to stop something or increase capacity. If you can, now is a good chance to outsource what you can to create literal capacity.

4. Similar to 2, those in leadership positions will have a heavier load, so underpin them with coaching or capability development.

5. Improved this one by learning about change as an organisation, by agreeing the consistent language and approach, a slightly more formal course or through the heaps of free learning that's available.

There's No Such Thing as Change Resistance, Just Terrible Change

Resistance to change is a symptom that something in your change isn't working, right or worth it. It's a massive red flag that you do not have this nailed. You can choose to worry about it, try to ignore it, get angry with it or you can accept that resistance to change is not terrible. We are conditioned to deal with, close down and 'manage' resistance. There are oodles of articles that list the cost of resistance in terms of delays, moral and ability to deliver. But we don't believe it, or at least we take it with half a gallon of salt. Because great things come from push back.

We already know that change is an individual phenomenon, its personal and so is resistance. The root cause for one person's resistance may not be the same as another person's because it depends on factors such as their value and beliefs, experiences and expectations. These are all unique and, therefore, almost impossible to second guess and debilitating if you choose to worry about them all. We aren't denying that resistance isn't a pain, we know it can be frustrating, but we choose to put it to work.

When our people demonstrate resistance, something is not right - it's a new and valid source of information that could improve your change process. If we look properly at what we are being shown, it is that certain aspects of a change are not being properly considered or aren't being considered in a way that resolves what people are worrying about.

There are usually 2 causes:

1. The change isn't right: this can be both perceived or evidenced. But the issue is with the proposal.

2. The way you're going about it doesn't work: this is often linked to speed, complexity and personal preference.

How do we use it to our advantage? Well first up, we don't declare to the resistance (or resistors) that we're looking for it to contribute to our change, to improve or influence what we are doing because we'll create all kinds of bonkers. However, when you are being hit with resistance don't just let it happen to you, engage with it, create space and let it make your change better:

```
                CREATE THE OPPORTUNITY TO EXPERIMENT
                                 |
    CO-CREATE                                      ADJUST
             \         WHEN HIT WITH         /
                         RESISTANCE
             /                               \
    SEEK EVIDENCE OR DATA                     LET GO
    THAT PROVES THE RESISTANCE
```

- **Seek evidence or data that proves the resistance** (the absence of it disproves the resistance, or at least makes it less credible, doesn't mean it won't be vocal though): this doesn't need to be empirical research but key facts, previous experiences and outcomes. This doesn't mean because 'last time we tried it, it didn't work' argument holds water, but learn from it, understand what went wrong and apply that learning to your change. Let the resistance improve what you are doing.

- **Co-create:** using any of the tools we have shared, bring your people together to share how you are going to do the things that need to be done. Resistance is your co-conspirator to sustainable and scalable change.

- **Create the opportunity to experiment**: most changes have more than one route, option or opportunity. So provide the opportunity to try a coupe of hypothesis or proof of concepts that can directly address areas of resistance.

- **Adjust:** sometimes it's 'just' too quick, unclear or complicated. So, listen and respond by making direct improvements and adjustments to your implementation plan. Small nudges towards preferences gives you both improved buy-in and the ability to put the resistance to work.

-

Let go: understand what you can control and what you can't, so do your best and leave the rest.

Resistance isn't there to be managed away, it is richness and curiosity. It can make your change better, it can make your people feel heard. And if it was you resisting what was happening around you, think about what you would need and want before you close down the conversation and shut up shop.

Er, Do We Not Plan Anymore?

A plan doesn't survive first contact with the enemy. That's what my dad would tell you. He always had one, he always knew his next move. He didn't plan, he had lived experience of the task in hand, of the human responses (and his own responses). He knew downfalls and rabbit holes that would appear 'out of nowhere'.

We probably all know, without the help of my dad, that planning is frustrating and ever changing, because people are people. And despite our mysterious ways we are pretty predictable. We can plan for the un-plannable, if we plan for people not robots.

And lots of the things you need to do this we have shared with you already.

- The task in Problem 3 asks you to breakdown your tasks into it's smallest components, this is your old school, work break down structure (eugh). You can sequence this.
- Your change goal map timeboxes the time in hand. You can align this to your tasks.
- Your benefits will keep you accountable for delivering for delivering the right outcomes. You can schedule reviews to see if you're on track.
- A Kanban will keep your change moving
- An improved understanding of your capability and capacity will tell you what you have to work with.

This is a responsive and flexible plan. It is everything you need.

If you are worried about taking these aspects forward as your plan to 'a board' you are probably engaging them too late in the process. So before you get knee deep in dashboards and status updates, talk to them about what they need, wha tis on offer and how it will work. By bringing them with you, they'll learn to work with it (or at least start to) rather than against it.

If you're retro-fitting your change to our approach, you can easily align your tasks with the timeboxes, calling out assumptions, risks and when you'll review your benefits. This will be closer to a more traditional plan, but built on foundations that start and end with your people.

What Happens if it Goes Up the Swanny

There's lots of theory that failure is a great learning device, should be welcomed, encouraged and supported. And I absolutely agree. There also lots of talk about 70% of changes failing with little or no evidence and with that we do not agree, if it wasn't frowned upon we'd probably show it the middle finger.

The tricky thing with failure, is it can be realised because your context isn't right or your change isn't optimised (rather than a gift from the Universe). But there could actually be a fundamental flaw with your plan to change. And there's a difference between something not going quite right, to something that could detrimentally impact your organisation or people.

If you think your change is actually going up the swanny (read: royally f*cked) – where the outcomes are likely to leave you in a worse place than where you have set off from or an unintended consequence has been brought to light, this is what I want you to do: take a breath. Literally breathe and slow down your thoughts.

I remember like it was yesterday, the first time a change I was in charge of went up the swanny. Everything about it was solvable but that feeling of my stomach dropping, heart rate kicking up a notch or two and some very sweaty palms means it's something I will never forget. Nobody else remembers it though.

It happens. It happens because change isn't perfect and controlled, it's a sequence of hypotheses at the whim of people (sounds great!). The control you can exert only reaches so far and you literally cannot know all the answers, predict outcomes or second guess everything that comes your way. You will eventually be able to spot issues or identify likely downfalls of your change as you do more, getting the reps in building your change muscles.

What you can do is identify the root cause – is the change wrong or the approach wrong or have we been slapped in the chops with a curve ball? Going back to the original change goal and the evidence that informed the decisions and the plans that followed will help you track back to see if something is adrift at the cause of change. You might want to re-visit some of the activities and tools we have covered so far (AHEM) to help you do this.

But for speed start by asking yourself:

1. Is your change still fit for purpose?

2. What is working well?

3. What are your blockers?

You might find the problem to be solved here. If not, **we can look at the implementation to see what's going on;**

1. What are you being told (and what are you hearing)?

2. How are your people feeling?

3. Are you coping (think organisational change load, systems, processes and constraints)?

Working through these questions and reflecting on where you are (honestly), might not mean you are able to pin-point the root cause to that email sent on a wet Wednesday but if you can get close to the cause you can look to resolve or move on.

When we know what has happened we can decide on what you want to do next. There are some relatively simple options:

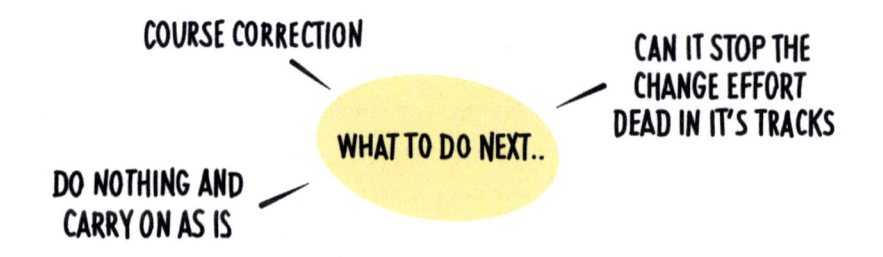

COURSE CORRECTION

CAN IT STOP THE CHANGE EFFORT DEAD IN IT'S TRACKS

WHAT TO DO NEXT..

DO NOTHING AND CARRY ON AS IS

1. **Do nothing and carry on as is** - this could be sensible if you disprove there was an issue, or you can isolate it and resolve it.

2. **Course correction** - vary the approach, change the scale of the change, re-prioritise. Maybe you can still deliver the change and intended out-

comes with a variation. It takes us right back to the start about knowing what your tolerances are, what are you willing to do to deliver?

3. **Can it**; stop the change effort dead in its tracks - this could be forever, or time boxed if the root cause needs significant time or correction. Its ok to stop change if its not getting you to where or what you need. It's not OK to mindlessly keep flogging a change because you said you would. It takes nerve to stop a change, it's likely that you'll need to make a case to stop especially if there's been investment, or the outcomes mitigate something risky or maximise a needed opportunity.

Stuff is going to go wrong, money will be wasted, time will be lost and yes, your ego will be bruised. But we create and curate change to improve where we are, to create new worlds and opportunities. So, make sure it's right, make it worth it and stay honest.

> AND ONE MORE TIME FOR THOSE AT THE BACK YOU CAN STOP YOUR CHANGE, IF IT'S NOT WORKING, NOT RIGHT, NOT VIABLE, YOU CAN AND PROBABLY SHOULD STOP

Not Everyone Needs to Love Your Change (be Involved, Like it or Even Care)

A bit of a change fable is that we think that everyone needs to be on the pitch, in the tent, around the table or on the bus. But, in all honesty, they don't. You need a critical mass but not necessarily everyone.

Hold up, isn't critical mass something to do with nuclear physics? Yes, yes it absolutely is. It started out as a term used to represent the smallest mass of material that can sustain a nuclear reaction. In change I use it to identify the amount of people, resource or buy-in where your change becomes viable, where it works in a way that is sustainable and scalable.

But what is your critical mass? When you think about and plan for your change, you need to understand the ground swell you need to create in order for this change to work for your organisation in the way that delivers you the best outcomes.

So, I give you the worst answer; it depends. And it is also an ever-changing target and not a constant one-time only goal, it's a guide that should grow, change or adapt with your organisation.

- If you are implementing a software solution and it requires a minimum number of users, this is your initial critical mass And when you have achieved it, or unlocked new functionality, your critical mass will increase to meet the next target.

- If you are introducing a new process to your total organisation and training is required to use it or understand it etc. then you'll need a higher mass than if it was affecting one group.

Focusing on a critical mass means you'll have enough to deliver the change without letting a minority derail your efforts. It also means that you can increase it, adjust it and come back for those who weren't 'included' the first time. You can come back with the evidence that the change is working and give it a final push to bring more people with you.

It doesn't mean you have picked a list of your favourite people and closed the door on everyone else, the change needs to remain open to everyone, but you are going to stop worrying about everyone, because that is thankless and will not get you progress.

The only time I'd caution the use of a critical mass above 'everyone' would be if you have a compliance or safety issue you may need to have 'everyone' affected or at least signed up to what is happening to either avoid something going wrong or a trip prison (because I cannot help you get out of prison).

Stakeholders Are Shit Stirrers

In most organisations stakeholders are there to be identified, put on a list and managed. We create entire strategies (read excel spreadsheets) on managing them. And let me be really clear, we manage them away from the change. We manage them to keep them quiet, appeased, satisfied. And stakeholders don't tend to like it. Because, more often the not, they care about what you are doing.

So, when you push them away, they push back. And as the management walls are high and tough. Rather than try and kick them down, they cause a bit of trouble, throw rocks, agitate, become shit stirrers to try and get you to listen to let them in.

Your agitated stakeholders will cause noise and disruption away from your change. Usually in two ways:

1. Shouting SQUIRREL and distracting you with contradictory data or problems

2. By accessing the apathetic or those colleagues that aren't really affected.

The second of these is the one to watch out for, as they start to create a shared cause, a united front for their frustration with your management approach, taking the shit stirring to level ten. And as they get louder, stronger and more convincing, you respond by managing harder. Sounds great, right?

You see, stakeholder management is an art and a science, like lots of change. There are some hard lines that you need to have and the rest is up for grabs. You have two options, manage harder (which I have never seen work well, but is sometimes funny to watch). Or let them in.

We choose to let them in, as the saying goes 'better to have your enemies inside the tent pissing out, than outside the tent pissing in'. And because we don't actually believe that stakeholders are enemies and we know good things come from constructive challenge, we suggest that you fill the tent, turn the heating on and get the tea bags out.

I also tell you this knowing that some people are better for your change than others, we explored this in the Able and the Willing. So, this isn't me asking, suggesting or telling you to make your change work for everyone. It's about letting your stakeholders find their place in your change; where they can contribute or pull some weight and letting them do so. Where they have questions, give them answers.

But where they aren't a good fit, let them go to avoid them being like little blocks of concrete holding on to your ankles and making everything feel shite, do it transparently and honestly, because you might need them next time.

It's Them

There's a chance that some of the *eugh* you are feeling is down to being accountable to a board, committee, management group etc. These are people who aren't often close enough to the detail to contribute with confidence, but are unsure enough to have a wobble and cast doubt (which I expect you'll then have a worry about). This usually happens in a public place or meeting and definitely when you don't have enough time or energy to respond, just to make the experience more fun.

DEALING WITH THE WOBBLERS...

Whilst I can't guarantee this will solve what you face, it will demonstrate that you want to improve their experiences, secure their support and that you know what you are doing:

1. **Be open to their objection, frustration or whinge-fest.** Talk about it until they can articulate what they need or what is missing. If they can't do that, I would suggest their response is one that reflects their ability and confidence, not yours.

2. **Ask for advice.** Seek guidance from your board (or challenger), give them a route in to share what they know (and probably what they're working on or worrying about) to give insight and to offer support or solutions. Be specific, asking 'how do we do all of this' will likely ensure panic, but focusing on a key delivery, risk or measure will focus the guidance rather than open you up to goodness knows what.

3. **Balance every solution with a problem or end every problem with a solution.** It is sometimes too easy to do something because it feels good, or opportune. But unless you know why you're doing it, whats its solving or where its taking you. your efforts are not going to get you progress and you're likely to lose support if your approach to changes feels like your chasing squirrels. Tie what you are doing to your strategy, desired outcomes or key risks. Make it real and then solve it.

4. **Talk in a way they understand.** It goes back to our earlier points on communications. Talk to them, not to you. Pitch to them, help them come with you by making it as easy as possible.

At the end of the day, they may never come round to it. But remember everyhting we have talked about, you don't need them all. Just enough to make it work.

What About the Change Curve?

Oh, how we laughed. I know this is a book about change and we have completely ignored one of the most used and cited models. Why? Because we simply do not like it. We don't like its history, its use and its influence on change.

> **BRIEF HISTORY: CHANGE CURVE WAS NOT ACTUALLY MEANT TO BE ABOUT ORGANISATIONAL CHANGE AT ALL**

It was developed by Elisabeth Kubler-Ross in the late sixties/early seventies and it was snappily titled Kubler-Ross Model for Death and Bereavement Counselling, Personal Change and Trauma. It focussed on the five stages of grief. It had never set foot into an organisation or office. Then, in the late nineties, Schneider & Goldwasser whipped it into the curve we know today based on correlations between their research and the model.

There is a really sensible argument against the change curve as a model. It lacks empirical evidence to support its assumptions and it fails to build understanding around the complexity of emotions and shared context as to why some people experience them during change. It also cops out and states that the 5 stages are neither sequential nor work in parallel, even though they are depicted as sequential and as pretty much essential.

It has legs because it means you can box your people and intervene based on a generic title of an emotion, which is great if you're selling a solution that solves those things. Less great if you are trying to support your people in a way that is meaningful to them.

The reason we don't like it, don't use it and don't advocate for it? Nobody or nothing gets to tell you how you feel.

Whether that's a partner, a boss or a mate, they aren't their feelings to pass comment on. So why does a management model get to do the same? It doesn't in our book (literally and metaphorically).

If you need a model to support your change journey go back to Bridges Transition Model. In those four walls you can move through your change in a way that works and means something for you. We think that is smashing. And if you want to travel without a model, five steps, a curve (you get my drift) just ask your people how they're feeling. Most of them will tell you.

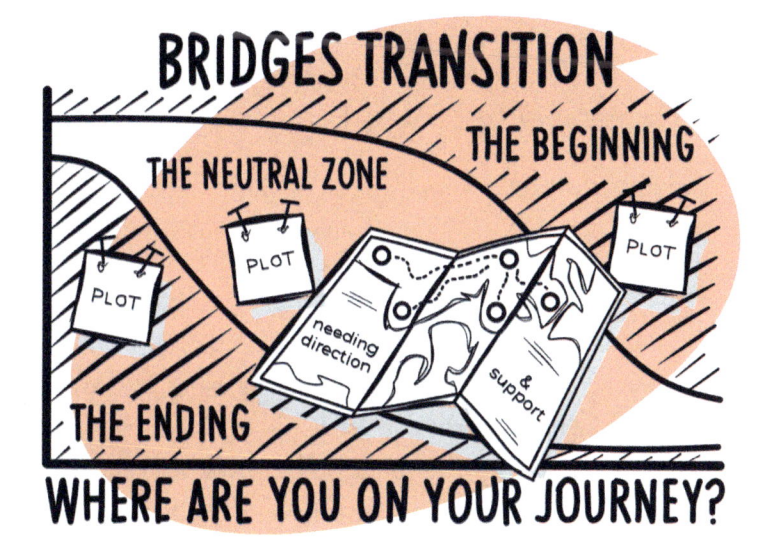

BRIDGES TRANSITION

THE NEUTRAL ZONE

THE BEGINNING

THE ENDING

PLOT

PLOT

PLOT

needing direction

& support

WHERE ARE YOU ON YOUR JOURNEY?

The Phenomenon of Resilience

This mega management buzzword is bandied around almost as much as resistance. The story for resilience is that it can enable your change to succeed.

We don't disagree that resilience is an asset and can improve experiences of those who 'have it'. If you want to help your organisation become better at change, the ability to weather the storm, roll with the punches etc. to have resilience when things feel off can really help you navigate change with a bit more confidence.

But there are myths that sit around what it actually means 'to be resilient' means. Resilience is not about accepting whatever happens blindly. Nor is it about "bouncing back" to how you were before the challenge or disruption occurred *as soon as possible so nobody notices*.

Resilience is about perseverance and problem-solving, being able to engage and make progress despite the setbacks and pressures. Resilience isn't about super positive happy change joy. Being ridiculously positive even when things are exploding around you, isn't being resilient, that's being in denial. Resilience is about seeing paths through, finding a way forward and accessing the support you need to make that progress.

So where does the resilience magic come from?

Resilience is often pitched as a 'you thing', where it's your responsibility and your fault when it's missing. But we think it's more of a team sport. Because resilience is not about you escaping a situation unharmed, but to enter into a change open to what's on the table, able to learn and make progress, in the best possible way based on your circumstances.

The change wouldn't be instantly easier/better if you were more resilient.

You do not go on a course to get sheep dipped in resilience.

Resilience needs to be nurtured, supported and encouraged. And one of the best ways to do that? With other people. Surround yourself by people and opportunties that can help that happen, that can help you learn and grow. Create this support infrastructure within your change and your people, give them the chance to be resilient and benefit from collective resilience of their friends, peers and colleagues. That is the resilience magic.

Everyone Else's Answers to Your Change Questions

Over the past 3 years we have repeatedly asked individuals and organisations questions about their change experiences. We do this beacuse we want to understand what the people we are working with have gone through. What do we need to be mindful of, where there might be fixed ideas and what they know (or think they know)?

And the biggest thing we have learnt, is what we are worrying about is never far from the next person or organisation. So we committed to keep them going. In part, to normalise conversations about how we change but also, to let you in on the secret that it's not always pretty, but it's also not as shit as it's often made out to be.

What follows is the outcomes of those conversations, games and stories we are privileged to be a part of. The answers are summarised where sensible but are truthful to the responses and sentiment from the people who said them. And naturally, we've let you know our opinion too.

WHAT WE ASKED: Who can lead change?

WHAT THEY SAID: Anyone. Everyone. I can. You. You. You. Me. We can. You. Me. Anyone who is ready. You. You. Those who want to. You. You. Anyone. Anyone. Me. All of us. Anyone.

THE EVERYDAY OPINION: The answer is still the same, anyone can lead. Your job title isn't a barrier. But you need to know why you are doing it and where you are aiming for.

WHAT WE ASKED: What can help you change?

WHAT THEY SAID: Time. The right people. Understanding what's needed. Knowing your organisation. Having a clear strategy. Being brave. The right capability for what you are doing. Patience. Clarity. A clear journey. Lots of patience. Clarity. Priorities. Actually getting started.

THE EVERYDAY OPINION: All true. And this book has been created to help you. You don't need to do it all, it doesn't need to be sequential but when you need something, it's here.

WHAT WE ASKED: When is change complicated?

WHAT THEY SAID: When we make it so. When we don't know our priorities. When we pretend it's all ok. Doing it all yourself. Lack of clarity. Rushing. When we are unsure of what we need so we try and solve everything. When we mess with stuff we shouldn't. If you disguise your intent. Pretending it's easy. Responding to optics. Making it fancier than it needs. Bad comms.

THE EVERYDAY OPINION: The biggest thing for us is when we pretend its all ok. You'll make it harder and you'll put your outcomes at risk. So talk about it, be clear about what you need and take it easy.

WHAT WE ASKED: How can you influence how your organisation changes?

WHAT THEY SAID: Ask questions. Be open. Willingness. Appreciative enquiry. Role model the behaviours you need. Challenge things that you are unsure of that make you uncomfortable. Speak up when you see great work or positive impacts. Calm down. Question the change. Share learning from elsewhere. Bring in help. Take the time to understand. Seek clarity. Offer support.

THE EVERYDAY OPINION: You can set the precedent as to what happens next. But work within your culture and values, make sure you are undoing or disregarding your shared beliefs and histories.

WHAT WE ASKED: When does change feel good?

WHAT THEY SAID: When it's understood. When it's timed well. Everyone is on the same page. Doesn't feel imposed. When I understand what is needed from me. Feeling supported. Expected. Kind. Clear. Sensible. Exciting. Ambitious. When I can see myself in it. Understood. Accessible. Open to Challenge. Confident. Responsive.

THE EVERYDAY OPINION: See, change doesn't need to be shit.

WHAT WE ASKED: When does change feel bad?

WHAT THEY SAID: When it's done to me.

THE EVERYDAY OPINION: The biggest barrier and hardest part to get right. So go with caution and openness and if you wouldn't like it if it was you on the receiving end, don't do it.

WHAT WE ASKED: What happens after change?

WHAT THEY SAID: Nothing. Stability. Calm. Learning. Growth. More change. Better decisions.

THE EVERYDAY OPINION: It's a lie that you have to carry on, so stop, slow down and stabilise. Oh and don't forget to celebrate.

WHAT WE ASKED: Do you need a change vision?

WHAT THEY SAID: Yes. Yes. No. Depends. It depends. Use your strategy? Yes. No. Maybe.

THE EVERYDAY OPINION: You need to know what you are doing and why. But it doesn't need a full-scale marketing campaign. Talk about your change in a way that your people will understand and in a way that will keep you honest.

WHAT WE ASKED: What makes a great change leader?

WHAT THEY SAID: Someone who understands the change. A good reputation. People who can listen. Someone who I recognise (doesn't always have to be 'the boss'). Relatable. Normal. The right capability and capacity to listen and lead. Stable yet passionate. Someone open to challenge and able to challenge. Respectful of the context and shared histories

THE EVERYDAY OPINION: Nothing fancy to see here, just someone trying to do their best by their people. Sound familiar?

WHAT WE ASKED: What happens when you fail?

WHAT THEY SAID: Learning. Growth. Some tears. Frustration. Better outcomes. Dust off and go again. Laughter. Changes to plans. Different approaches. A chance to reflect. Understanding what went wrong. Trying it a different way.

THE EVERYDAY OPINION: No explosions. We have already covered this.

WHAT WE ASKED: Does change have to be perfect?

WHAT THEY SAID: No. No. Nada. Not really. Maybe. No. No. Fit for purpose. No. No. Useful/usable. Progressive.

THE EVERYDAY OPINION: Setting off searching for perfect is like looking for the crock of gold at the end of the rainbow. Set your sights on 80% and start to reign it in when 70% is on the table.

WHAT WE ASKED: How would you change for the better?

WHAT THEY SAID: Better clarity. Understanding the ripple effect. Talking about it more. Normalise it. Make it a focus. Build capability. Ask for help. go slower. More confidence. Calm. Smaller chunks. Focussed on the here and now. More local. People lead. Without as much worry. Break it down. Understand what 'enough' is. Don't change everything at once. Know priorities.

THE EVERYDAY OPINION: In a way that works for you and your people.

WHAT WE ASKED: What is the most important thing when changing?

WHAT THEY SAID: Breathing.

THE EVERYDAY OPINION: Yep.

WHAT WE ASKED: Are you ready to lead change?

WHAT THEY SAID: Yes. Probably. Yes. Not yet. With support. Yes. OK.

THE EVERYDAY OPINION: Of course you are. You might need some help, but it's all there.

The End

If you are here you are probably one of two people. The ones that start at the end to see if the answer is in the final chapter or the ones who have actually read it from top to bottom. Whichever one you are, I am glad you're here.

We have covered a lot. I hope we have covered it in a way that has taken away some of the busyness and bluster that often gravitates toward change. I hope you are feeling more able.

I doubt you'll ever use everything we have shared here. In fact, I hope you don't. Why? Not because it's not smashing but because the book was never supposed to dictate a path or approach. It is here to help you deliver a change that you can get on board with in a way that respects you and your people.

I wanted to use this book to create space and hold space for you so you have time to think or swear. I wanted to show you how, give you ways to move forward and on the days needed, give you the back-up you need that reminds you the madness is temporary. Most importantly, I wanted to end where we began, with you. Change is personal.

I expect that your change road ahead will be bumpy. My dear, it should be. Change is disruptive and discombobulating. Find a flow that works and go with it. Look for resistance and bring it in. Let it keep you honest. Create change that enables you to participate as an individual and for your people. Your change will be better if you create the time and space to do it 'properly' and with meaning.

If you are reading this book and you don't have a change breathing down your neck, I hope it has sparked some intrigue in how change comes about and what it can both create and break. I hope you get to take something away that improves your outlook or experiences both as an individual, a leader and a spectator. When your time comes, be openly creative and ambitious in what you do, because change doesn't need to be shit.

So, What Next?

Breathe. Go for a walk. Reflect.

Everything I have written down and shared with you is designed to make your change better or, more accurately, *less shit*. Despite writing a book full of useful and occasional witty change based deliciousness, I know it's tough. My ambition is to help you change your world in a way that respects your shared histories, context and culture. I can't do the latter part in a book, this sits with you. Before you put this book down, think about that. Think about the rich tapestry of your world and your people. Remind yourself of it and of them. What happens next will happen in that world. Don't forget what it feels like.

My closing caveat is that there is more out there than this book. There will be things you'll need to know more of, less of and new things that emerge over time. There will be days when you need more than a book, you'll need support from an actual human. Invest in that support. If it's me and Everyday Change, we'd be over the moon to be with you on your journey. If it's not us, we're good with that too. We know you need to choose what and who you need in order to get you where you are going.

As you're about to close this book, I want to remind you to be open. Be open to change, to feedback, to conversations, to getting it wrong, to saying well done, thank you and sorry. Be open to your own growth and your own story.

Change is as soft and gentle as you need or as fast and wild as you want. It will be brimming with opportunity.

Hold your nerve.

Go with confidence.

I cannot wait to see what you do.

What Do You Now Know and When to Use it

Here we consolidate all of the tools we have shared into your tool kit. This section focusses on the tools we have shared away from the 3 problems. We'll tell you when to do this during your change, how to get the most out of it and some of the things to watch out for. Most of these tools work best when done at the start and then revisited. So, if you are already knee deep in your change, pick out the tools that can give you confidence rather than point out what is missing.

When you read this section you might feel there isn't enough here. There is. As we said, it's not necessarily what you do but how you do it. Everything else you need, you have, because it's you.

Theory of Change

When to use it: this is great at the start as part of your approvals process. It will tell you whether you have a change that can hold its own and whether it is worth the effort. It challenges you to know what you are doing, why and what with (and this is harder than you might imagine!). It is not a business case but it will provide enough context, ambition and outcome to support a financial or resource request. It is your total change on one page.

You can use any template to create yours. We've included ours so you can have a go, but 5 minutes in your nearest search engine will give you fancier ones if you need.

Things to watch out for: it assumes you know the resources you need to do what you are suggesting. If you don't, assume that your ability to deliver is bound by what you have now, not what you might have later. It is also a tool used a lot by charities or not-for-profits which can be a blocker if your decision makers can't draw a comparison or get past that.

THEORY OF CHANGE

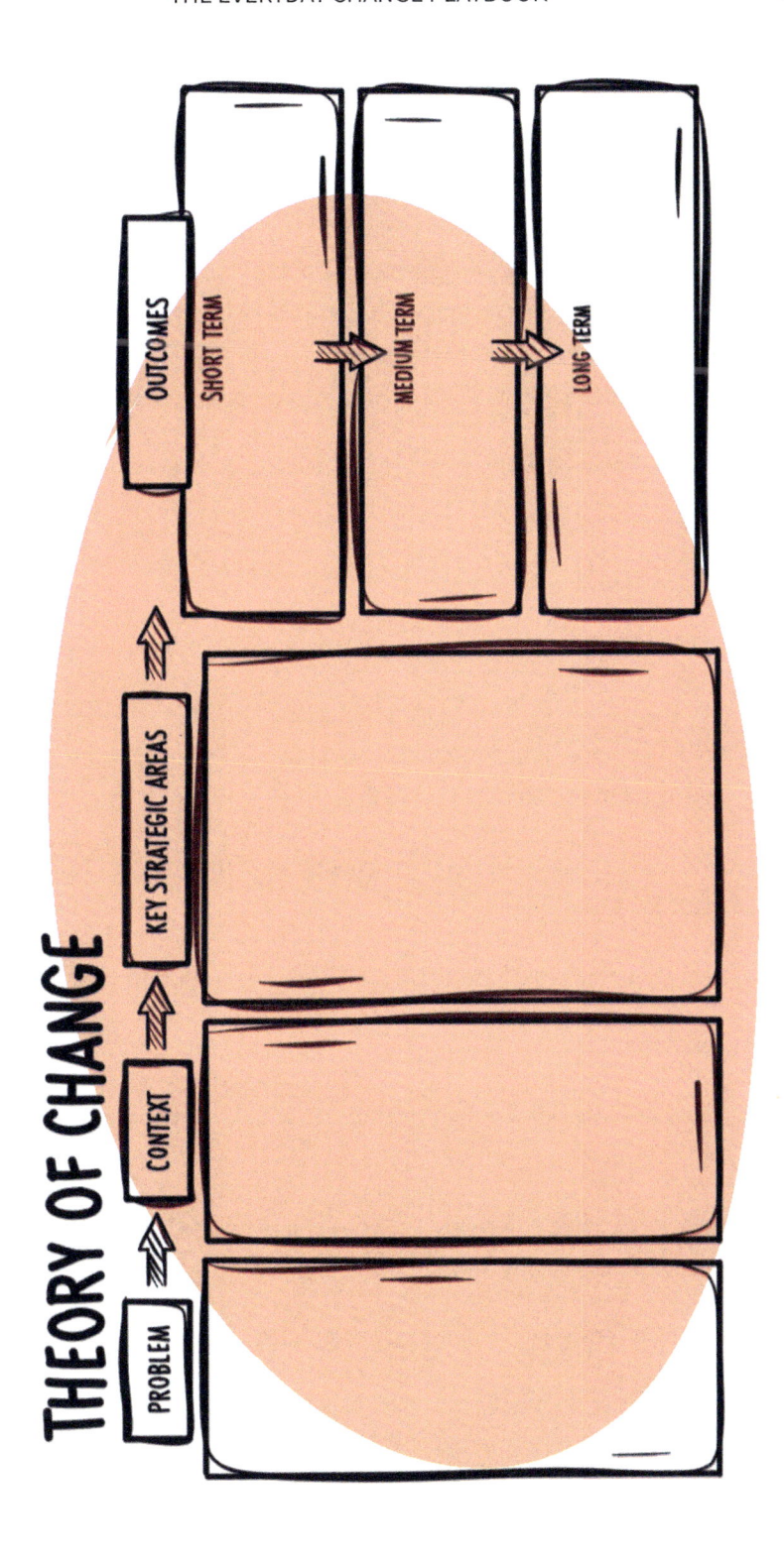

PROBLEM

CONTEXT

KEY STRATEGIC AREAS

OUTCOMES
- SHORT TERM
- MEDIUM TERM
- LONG TERM

Bridges Transition Model

When to use it: the very premise of the Transition Model is as soon as you start to end, you have begun on your journey. As soon as you start talking about your change you are trying to get people to commit to 'endings'. Get this one in use from the start as a tool for early engagement, helping your people find their place in your change. You can use it to shape what you are doing or as a prompt for how you can support your people. Everything we know about Bridges is because we have used it and researched it. If you want to know more: www.wmbridges.com

I have included some of the 'things' you might want to consider as prompts to get you using it.

The Ending

- Make space to talk about what is changing, why its happening and what remains the same.

- Create genuine opportunity for people to express their views, concerns and frustrations. Be prepared to listen.

- Find a way to signal the 'end', respecting all of the great stuff and getting ready for a new way.

- Identify actions that can create momentum and start the process.

The Neutral Zone

- Share what you know when you know it to avoid creating an echo chamber.

- Be open to doing differently. seek out opportunities to help you and your people find their way through the change.

- Set short term goals to demonstrate progress.

- Remain open to changing course, pace or approach.

The New Beginning

- Prepare for the new world by providing training, support and psychological safety for people to try new things, learn and grow.

- Enable those who have made their transition to lead, support and encourage others to follow.

- Set longer term goals focussed on how you will sustain, improve and get benefits from the new world.

Things to watch out for: it doesn't always translate well as an en masse tool. If you have a hefty organisation, you will probably be better off using some of our notes and ideas to support folk moving through the phases rather than asking them to point at it and tell you where they are.

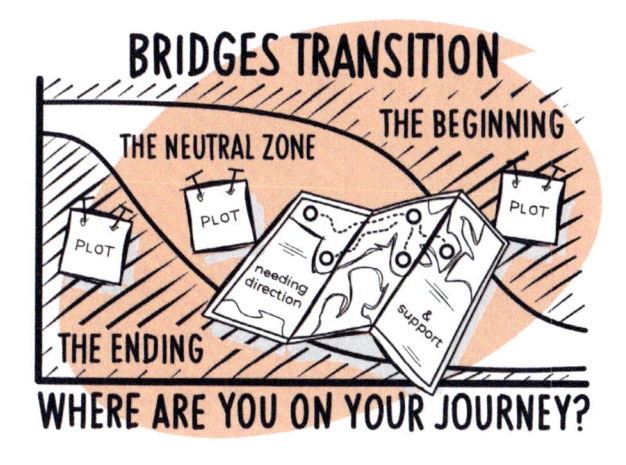

BRIDGES TRANSITION

THE NEUTRAL ZONE
THE BEGINNING
THE ENDING

WHERE ARE YOU ON YOUR JOURNEY?

Change Goal Mapping

When to use it: when you are ready to plan. This is great way to help you set your course away from dates, use change ambition you have and start to build your plan toward it. You want to create timeboxes that work for you, based on your change. We'd opt for 3 but you might need 12. Aligning people, process and products to your change. If one doesn't fit or you want to call it something else, go for it. As we said its more about the feelings and less about the deliverables, We aren't looking for details on the progress of your widgets. We want rich stories about your change and your people. This is all about them.

Things to watch out for: talking about how things feel can be weird. You will need to set some parameters to avoid it being personal, triggering and to make it accessible (lots of people will not be used to talking about how it feels). You may want to write everything in the 3rd person or by group. Whilst change is personal, sometimes writing it on a post it and putting it on a wall can feel a step too far.

CHANGE GOAL MAPPING
TRACK & TRACE YOUR CHANGE GOAL

1 2 3

PEOPLE

PRODUCTS

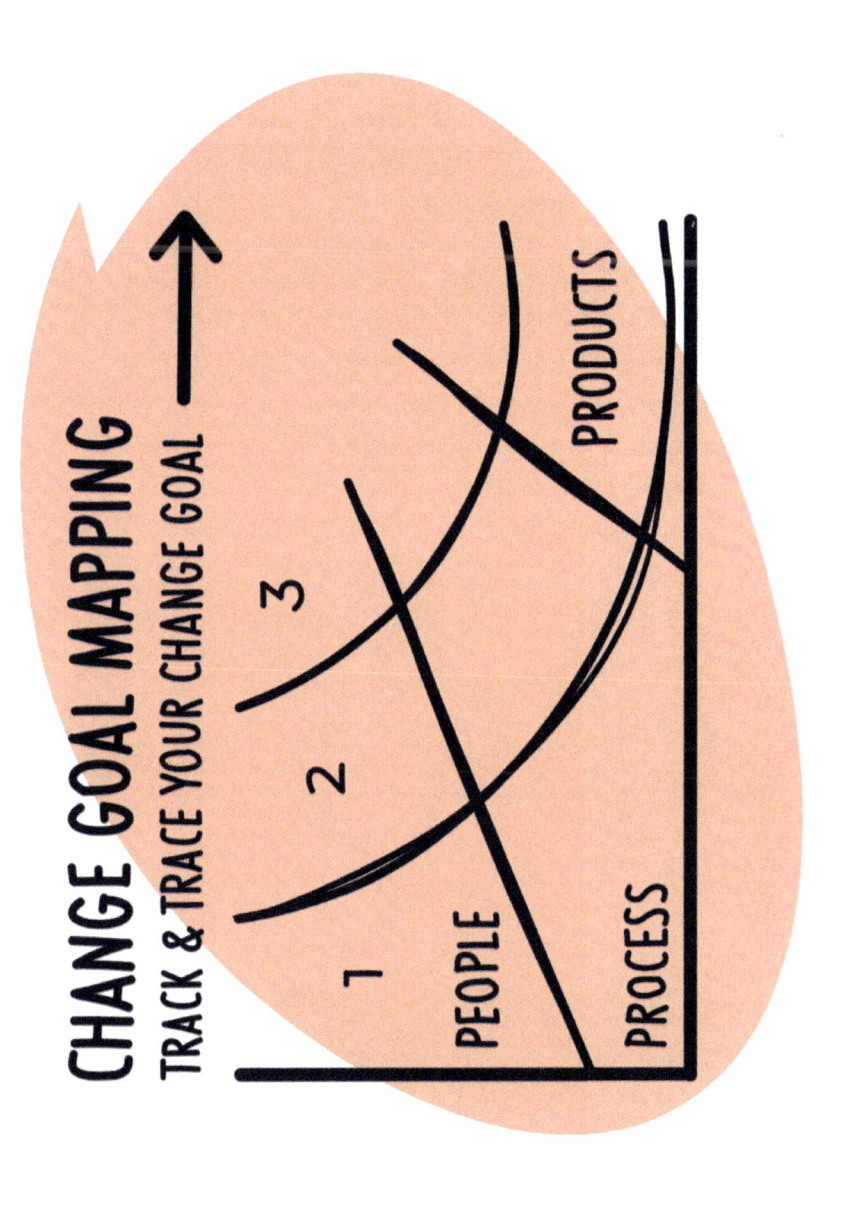

PROCESS

Change On a Page

When to use it: when you are ready to start to bring your people into your change. It is a wonderful engagement tool as well as being practical and actionable. Use it to help create individual and team narratives. You can use it for your organisation or at a team level. Whilst we advocate for consistency when you use this tool, you can use it to drill down into more localised details

Things to watch out for: what happens in the room can be read as agreed or 'done'. When you have had your conversations about the change and your page is drafted, revisit it to make sure it accurately represents where you are and that there is a shared understanding. If there isn't then you risk folk running off in the other direction with different adventures in mind. If you are using it at organisational and team levels, make sure everyone starts with the same objective to make sure that your individual pages are all from the same book.

CHANGE-ON-A-PAGE

VISION

WHAT WILL GOOD LOOK LIKE?	HOW WILL WE KNOW WE ARE GETTING THERE?

WHO IS IMPACTED?	WHAT IS IMPACTED?

HOW WILL WE SUPPORT THE CHANGE?

WHAT WILL HAPPEN?

NOW	NEXT	LATER

4 Boxes

When to use it: whenever you need some breathing space. Tip: grab a piece of paper and work out what you are up against. Don't bin the piece of paper, keep it with you so it can help you and your decisions.

Things to watch out for: it needs discipline. Doing it once won't mean you're all fine in 6 months. You'll need to revisit it and enable it to help you.

	STRATEGIC	TACTICAL/BAU
OPPORTUNITY		
PROBLEM		

Benefits

When to use it: benefits will be part of your conversations from the start, whether that's through Theory of Change, Change on a Page or just a 'normal' business case. So you are sure you know why you're doing what you're doing. Our approach is a great way (we would say that!) for helping everyone in or affected by the change to see what they'll get or where they might benefit. Having Benefits to track will help you you stay on course, celebrate early wins (or any wins) and are a good sign that if you aren't achieving them something is off.

Things to watch out for: emperors new clothes. This is where you tell yourself that you are achieving the benefits, but you aren't or, at least, not in the way you planned. So, rather than stand there starkers, call it out when it doesn't feel right so you can revisit, reset and make sure the change is still the change you needed. The one thing we haven't really spoken about is that sometimes the outcomes of a change is bad news for individuals. They will not have or see the benefits you see. Don't labour it, let them be and see if they need any support.

Kanban

When to use it: you'll set this up at the start but it will run the lifecycle of your change. Talk around it and be active in its role in your priorities and work. Spend time working through how much work you can handle because you will not get it right the first time. Look out for what causes issues and blockers, find solutions, implement them and go again. Let the decision makers help you learn and spot issues. Use them to get the flow of work right for you and your change.

Things to watch out for: forgetting it is there. You need to use it for it to work. That's as complicated as this one gets.

Writing is Never a Solo Affair.

This isn't a heartfelt page of acknowledgements. It's a list of thanks love, for the people who helped get this here.

Family P-T for never complaining to my standard response of 'I'm nearly there, just one more minute' and waiting patiently for the millions to start rolling in.

Jan, for your early feedback *'yeah, it's alright actually'* and for sticking with it to share her insights on resilience and storytelling, and who took great delights in pointing out every typo, ever.

Liam, for bringing this book to life in a way that goes beyond what I imagined at a time when your family became a three. For more: www.leodo.co.uk

Lisa, for making sure it actually got written and knowing that deep down I do need compliments, so lead with 'I think it's pretty smashing' before pointing out the half-finished sentences in draft one. It was downhill from there, so direct any complaints to her please www.makeyourcopycount.com

And you. Whether this is a mistake, a Christmas present, you're my mate, a client, the competition. Thank you. Not for the £3 I'll receive for the book you have in your hands, but for being open to a different way of change and for helping me fulfil my ambition to change worlds.

So. Thanks love.

About Us

Everyday Change is not-quite-a consultancy. Why? Because it has all the talent and none of the fuss, with an open optimism that your experiences of change can be positive and should always be centred around being *better*. And the best bit? It's all about you.

Everyday Change provides change management and leadership capability to organisation when they need it most. It is built on 15 years of experience delivering complex change, creating (and curating) strategy and building capability across organisations of all sizes; underpinned by accredited and credible learning.

We created Everyday Change after becoming bored and frustrated with engaging with the 'Big 4' of seeing what happened (or didn't) in their blast radius. Tired of slide decks, sausage machine solutions and for not getting to the heart of our people or our problems. For not caring enough about some of the most important things that were rippling through our organisations.

Everyday change is built on the premise of making change better, or more accurately *less shit*. Because we know it's tough. Our ambition is to help you change your world, in a way that respects your shared histories, context and culture.

We believe change should be:

Easier: change is complex. We know. But there's no need for it to be complicated, confusing or unfair. There's a great opportunity for us to err on the side of simplicity when it comes to delivering change and in doing so the outcomes will be better.

Better: you should always have the end goal of being better than the place you started. Not revolutionary transformation, just better.

Done: quite literally change should end. Change needs to end to give it time to embed, flex, grow, shift. And your people need time to stop, reflect and breathe

In 2022 we set a goal to write down everything we know about change. What we have learnt, explored and understood. This book is that goal achieved. There's more out there than this book, of course there is. This is us honouring our promise to share it, learn from it and to help make your change, better.

You can find out more about us here everyday-change.com

Susie Palmer-Trew

Change has been my world for as long as I can remember. But it took me a fair while to get it right, to try and not fix it all. Everyday Change was created because I know there has to be a better was of changing, of getting this stuff right, of taking away some of the drama and bluster. So that is what I do. I partner with organisations to make change easier. I enable people like you to create change that works for your people and your organisation.

My favourite things to work on are things that make my face hurt; complex ideas and ambition that need both the care and courage to have the impact you want them to have. I will challenge you and cheer for you in equal measure, your change will become mine and when we are done, I'll get my handbag and I'll go, still rooting for you to continue succeeding, growing and laughing.

And then I go home to my family, where I am a Wife and Mama, Chief Lego Piece Finder and reacher of things on the tallest shelf. Happy head, happy heart.

Jan Jayes

I have worked in both the public and private sectors, in roles within sales, marketing, business development, risk, project management and change management. A qualified change management practitioner, change has been my focus for several years, most notably working at The Open University as part of the award-winning Portfolio Office Team.

My favourite thing about change is the power of communities and storytelling in terms of how they simply make your change more accessible, real and generally better. I love exploring the psychology of change, and how it relates across disciplines, organisations and people.

My world starts with my husband and son in Milton Keynes (but originally from Birmingham so my Brummy twang runs strong) and I hang out with Everyday Change as a consultant working with people like you, to make change, less shit.

If you'd like to find out how Everyday Change can support your change adventure you can head this way everyday-change.com

Printed in Great Britain
by Amazon